NEWCASTLE PRISON

A HISTORY 1828 - 1925

PATRICK LOW, SHANE MCCORRISTINE,

HELEN RUTHERFORD AND CLARE SANDFORD-COUCH

© Patrick Low, Shane McCorristine, Helen Rutherford and Clare Sandford-Couch

ISBN: 978-1-7392233-5-9

All rights reserved. No part of this book may be reproduced, stored or introduced into a retrieval system or transmitted in any way or by any means (electronic, mechanical, photocopying, recording or otherwise) without the prior permission of the publishers.

The opinions expressed in this book are those of the authors.

Published by:
City of Newcastle Upon Tyne
Newcastle Libraries
Tyne Bridge Publishing, 2025

Layout design Derek Tree.

AUTHOR BIOGRAPHIES

Dr Patrick Low specialises in the history of execution and post-mortem punishment in the North East of England. He is a published academic author and freelance expert for the BBC's *Murder, Mystery and My Family* and a web designer. In 2022 he developed, with Dr Shane McCorristine, an online history of Newcastle Gaol.

Dr Shane McCorristine is Reader in Cultural History at Newcastle University specialising in the history of crime, exploration, and the supernatural. He is a Fellow of the Royal Historical Society and his books include *William Corder and the Red Barn Murder: Journeys of the Criminal Body* (2014) and *The Spectral Arctic: A History of Dreams and Ghosts in Polar Exploration* (2018).

Dr Helen Rutherford is an Associate Professor in the Law School at Northumbria University. She is a qualified solicitor. Her historical research interests include the nineteenth century coroner and crime, trials, and punishment - with a North East England focus. She is the editor (with Clare Sandford-Couch and Patrick Low) of *Execution Culture in Nineteenth Century Britain- From Public Spectacle to Hidden Ritual* (2020).

Dr Clare Sandford-Couch is an Associate Lecturer in the Law School at Leeds Beckett University. A solicitor and a legal academic for over 20 years, Clare has published on legal history and visual culture, and criminal legal histories in North East England in the nineteenth century. She is currently researching policing and detection in nineteenth century Newcastle.

NOTE TO THE READER

'Gaol' is an older spelling of 'jail', and is pronounced in the same way. The spelling was standard in British English until the second half of the twentieth century. Although commonly referred to as Newcastle Gaol, during its short history the prison was known by many different names both officially and colloquially, and inconsistently. These include Newcastle Upon Tyne Borough Gaol and House of Correction, Newcastle Upon Tyne Borough Gaol, Newcastle-upon-Tyne Prison, Her Majesty's Prison Newcastle, HMP Newcastle-upon-Tyne, Carliol Square Gaol and Carliol Street Prison.

In the text we use Gaol when writing about the institution prior to 1877, and then use Prison to reflect the change of name following the transfer of oversight from the local council to the Prison Commission.

ACKNOWLEDGEMENTS

This book is a collaboration by four historians who share interests in the history of Newcastle and the history of crime and execution. A serendipitous set of circumstances allowed us to bring these general interests together to research the history of Newcastle Prison. When we first began our research we were concerned that there would not be enough extant archival or primary sources to support a book, and that there would not be general interest in a nineteenth-century prison that has long since disappeared. How wrong we were! We now realise that we have merely scratched the surface of the history of Newcastle Prison and that people are curious to learn about how this building operated, who was incarcerated there, and its role in the story of Newcastle.

We could not have completed this work without the support, guidance, and expertise of many people, institutions, and funders. We acknowledge and thank: Tyne and Wear Archives, NEM (especially Lizzy Baker and Rachel Grahame); City Library, Newcastle (especially Sarah Mulligan and Andrew Scrogham); New Visions Heritage (especially Iwan Peverett); Northumberland Archives; Durham Record Office; National Archives, London; Newcastle University Library; Newcastle City Council (especially Tony Daly-Brand and Simon Parkin); School of History, Classics and Archaeology, Newcastle University; Northumbria University Library; Northumbria University Law School; The Literary and Philosophical Society; Potts Print (UK) Ltd; Derek Tree at Tyne Bridge Publishing; Dr Julie Young; Megan Adams; and Lorna MacKay. The research in this book was supported by the following Newcastle University funds: a Catherine Cookson Foundation Award, the Engagement and Place Fund, and the Dean's Discretionary Fund.

July 2025

CONTENTS

CHAPTER 1: INTRODUCTION — 10

CHAPTER 2: LIFE INSIDE — 32

CHAPTER 3: PRISON STAFF — 59

CHAPTER 4: THE WOMEN'S GAOL — 85

CHAPTER 5: ESCAPES — 104

CHAPTER 6: EXECUTIONS — 125

CHAPTER 7: BURIAL & POST-MORTEM PUNISHMENT — 153

CHAPTER 8: DEMOLITION AND BEYOND — 176

CHAPTER 1

INTRODUCTION

On 26 November 1919 the last person to be executed in Newcastle upon Tyne was led to a shed, hidden from the public, within the high walls of the city centre prison located in Carliol Square, east of Pilgrim Street. At 9.15am, executioner John Ellis pulled the bolt on the scaffold and 28-year-old Ambrose Quinn was hanged by the neck. Quinn was the second man to be executed that morning - Ernest Bernard Scott, also aged 28, was hanged at the stroke of 8am. Quinn was a corporal in the Royal Air Force who murdered his wife after suspecting she had been unfaithful to him during his service. Scott also killed a woman he knew, but unlike Quinn, he confessed to the crime and welcomed his death. Both men died instantly. After a while, a prison warder emerged to post a notice on the entrance door to formally record that the executions had taken place. The warder retreated and the iconic prison gates, stained black with almost 100 years of grime and coal dust, shut - and so ended the gruesome ceremony. Both men were buried in unmarked graves in the prison yard.

Scott and Quinn were not typical Newcastle inmates. There were an estimated 250,000 commitals to the prison during its operation and the most common prisoner was a young working-class man aged in his 20s who worked as a labourer, was born in Northumberland, and was convicted of larceny or other minor offences. Of course, this generalisation disguises the diversity of inmates, their offences, nationalities, and prison experiences. The formidable gates to the Prison opened for boys and girls arrested for theft; clerks guilty of fraud; drunk and disorderly seamen from all corners of the globe; and countless ordinary citizens in debt. Political and military prisoners were rare, although the prison housed suffragettes in 1909, German internees during World War I, and republican activists during the Irish War of Independence. As a local prison, sentences were usually short - typically several months of hard labour.

The executions of Scott and Quinn in 1919 were the last to take place in Newcastle; and less than six years later the prison was closed, the buildings demolished, and a telephone exchange built on the site. The buried bodies from the yard had to be removed and in 1925 newspapers reported that several skeletons were disinterred and driven, under cover of darkness, to All Saints Cemetery, Jesmond, where they were buried in secret in an unmarked plot. This burial symbolises the history of the Prison in Newcastle. Gone, yet not quite erased - a story of crime and punishment, but also a story of a city dealing with the past, whilst being unable to fully bury it.

This book developed out of a recent revival in interest in the history of Newcastle Prison. Since 2020 we have investigated the history of the prison and its legacy, creating a website and researching with the support of archivists, artists, designers and librarians. In 2022 and in 2025 we curated a public exhibition in Newcastle City Library and were delighted to see so many people attend and learn - in many cases for the first time - about the Prison. We have since noted how the history of the Prison inspires people to think about the way Newcastle manages to radically reinvent its urban fabric every few generations. Even a relatively small area like that east of Pilgrim Street has become unrecognisable in the past 10 years - demolished by the wrecking

Reconstruction of Newcastle Prison as first built.

ball are the Art Deco landmarks of Carliol House, the Dex Garage, and the (perhaps less beloved) Worswick Street bus station. Newcastle Prison should be a part of conversations about the role of planners in re-shaping this layered city over the past 200 years.

We have been contacted by several descendants of the people who spent time at Newcastle Prison, whether as staff or as prisoners. We heard stories from them of dramatic escapes, legendary underground tunnels, and the final words of condemned men. For us, sharing these stories of the Prison is a way of bringing the richly layered history of East Pilgrim Street back to life, as another cycle of regeneration threatens to disturb it.

Surviving images of some of the prisoners are held by North East Museums. This is John Roman (age 64), c.1873.

Photographs of two young prisoners held in Newcastle Prison. Patrick O'Neill (19) and Rosanna Watson (13).

Crime and Punishment in Newcastle

Newcastle is rich in the history and heritage of crime and punishment. From the hanging of 15 alleged witches on the Town Moor in 1650 to the execution of the notorious train carriage murderer John Dickman in 1910, the city has its fair share of tales of death and violence. Newcastle's three gallows sites - on the Town Moor; outside the old town gate at Westgate; and the prison in Carliol Square - each tell stories of the town's expansion and urban development, as well as changing attitudes to capital punishment.

A depiction of the execution of witches on the Town Moor, from Ralph Gardiner's Englands Grievance Discovered.

By the beginning of the nineteenth century, there had long been concern among the town's authorities that the main prison - Newgate - was not fit for purpose and had become a school for criminals. The key problem was that prisoners, old and young, male and female, mingled and communicated with each other while they waited to be tried, fined, or physically punished. This situation hindered efforts at reform or learning. As a newspaper editorial of 1822 put it:

'The young and the simple departed from their cells initiated in all the artifice and trickery of accomplished villainy, and, in many instances, the petty pickpocket soon returned to the scene of his instructors in the more important character of a highway-man or a house-breaker.'

Given Newgate's proximity to the town's outer limits and Northumberland beyond, it was tempting for prisoners to attempt to escape from Newgate and make for the fields beyond Gallowgate. Indeed, in 1800, three prisoners escaped by making a hole in the chimney of their cell, climbing onto the roof, and descending by a rope made from bed clothes. A fourth prisoner, of a more corpulent build, became stuck in the chimney and could neither get down nor up until he was assisted by the warders. Any felons who died in Newgate, or were executed on the Town Moor, were buried on the north side of the churchyard of St Andrew's: when Gallowgate was excavated for widening in the 1890s local antiquarians discovered corroded iron fetters amid the human remains.

Across Britain, in the 1820s, local authorities, magistrates, politicians, and philosophers debated the question: what is the purpose of a prison? Was it to punish or reform offenders? A great reform movement started to emerge in prison policy which centred on the 'classification system' - a new philosophy whereby prisoners were to be physically separated according to type - women, children, debtors, male offenders, and serious offenders. Inmates would sleep in single cells that were elevated in the building and they would have minimal contact with fellow prisoners. This combination of isolation, silence, and order was intended to provoke self-reflection and to encourage prisoners to reform by solitary work and without the distraction of any negative influences. In design terms, this meant that new prisons were planned with a central set of buildings observing radial wings that could be controlled and separated from the whole if need be. An extreme manifestation of this philosophy was the 'panopticon', a means of controlling inmates via surveillance that was first developed by the liberal theorist Jeremy Bentham.

THE NEWGATE PETITION

An engraving of the demolition of Newgate in 1823.

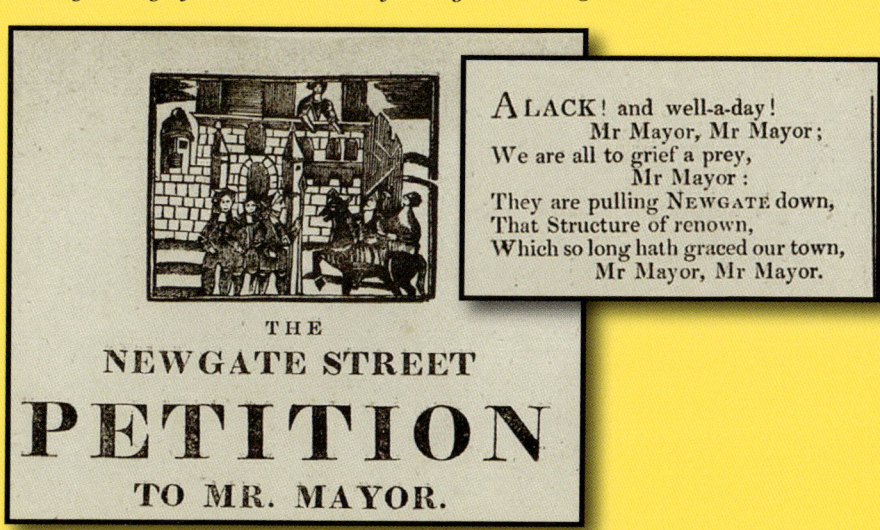

The Demolition of Newgate prompted the publication of a 'Petition' to the Mayor which included these lines.

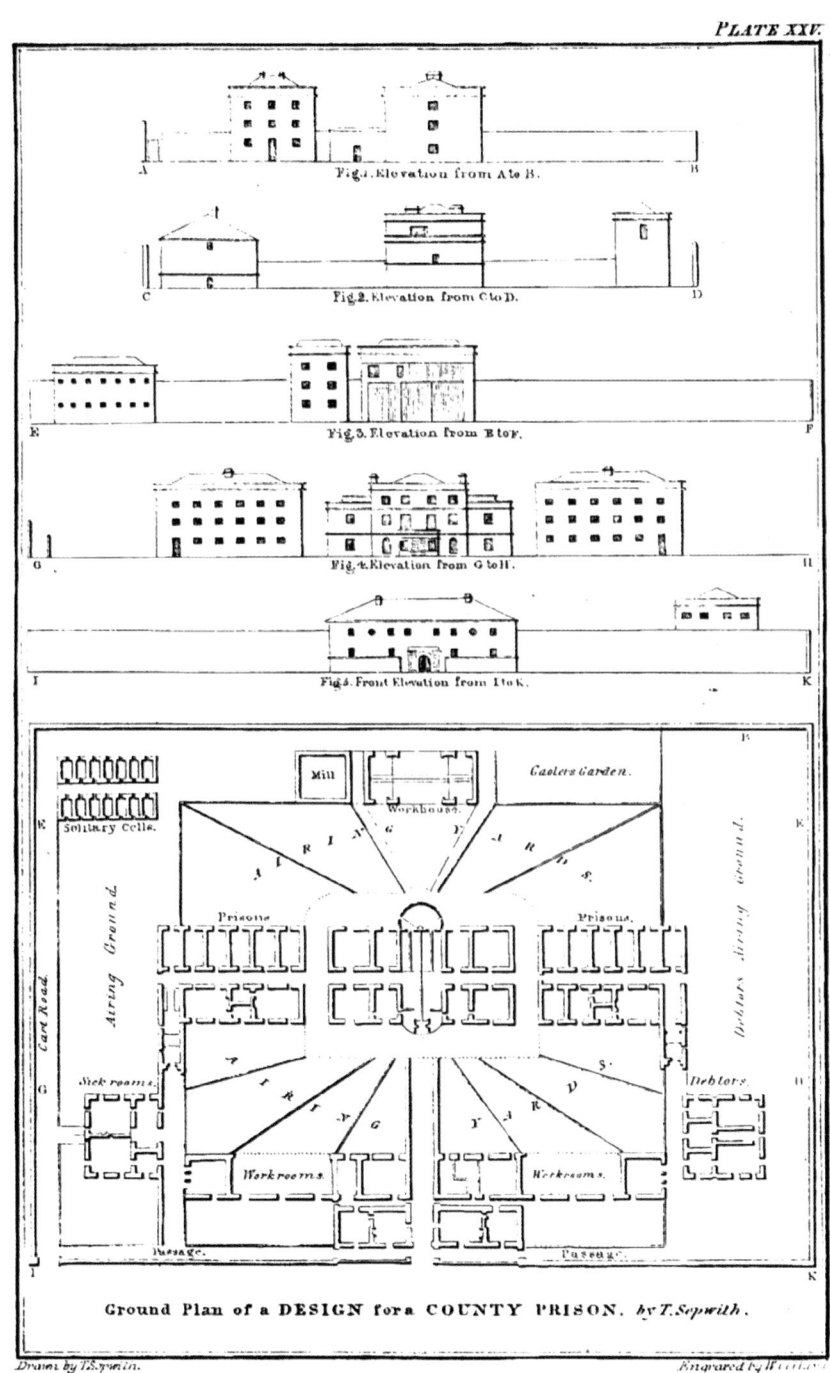

Suggested design for County Prison by T. Sopwith (not adopted).

The Birth of Newcastle Gaol

Following an Act of Parliament in 1822, authorities in Newcastle were given the green light to build a new gaol that could provide a modern and reform-minded approach to criminal justice. This was in line with the civic vision of Newcastle's town councillors in the 1820s and 30s, who were bankrolling ambitious building schemes such as the Moot Hall, Leazes Terrace, Grey Street and the developments that are now known as Grainger Town. Newgate prison was in such a state that it was demolished in 1823 before the replacement had been built, much to the consternation of the antiquarians who wrote a comic petition for its survival.

While Newcastle's criminals and debtors were temporarily housed in the basement of the Moot Hall and dungeon of Castle Garth, the innovative plans of John Dobson (1787-1865), Newcastle's stellar architect, were accepted by the authorities, following a competition which attracted three entries.

Although the Castle had been mooted as a location for a gaol, the town authorities chose to purchase a two acre site on Carliol Croft, a large area of ground within the town walls that stretched from Carliol Tower to Corner Tower on the east side of the town. This location made sense as it was an undeveloped site east of Pilgrim Street - Newcastle's main artery - and north of an area already hosting several related institutions, including the old house of correction, several hospitals, the Barber Surgeons' Hall, the poor house, and a charity school. However, the plot of ground was on an incline down to the Manors and was considered clayey and 'objectionable' by commentators. Furthermore, the area north of the proposed gaol site was in the midst of gentrification in 1823, with Dobson building himself a house on nearby New Bridge Street. The confined location of the Gaol, with no room to expand amid the busy districts around Carliol Square, would prove to be the main factor in its unsuitability as a long-term prison.

Charles Hutton's 1770 Map of Newcastle showing the Carliol Croft site.

Dobson's plan was to create an imposing prison with a fortress-style central tower, formidable arched gateway and door, and over 100 cells, the window of each looking onto the blank wall of another wing. The plan was in line with Bentham's panopticon ideal and it envisaged six radiating wings leading to an elliptical building in the middle. Each wing had its own exercise space, sick room, and water-closet that 'can never emit any offensive or unhealthy smell'. Female prisoners and debtors were given their own wings. Prisoners would pass through boundary walls that were 24.6 feet [7.5 metres] wide and enter the Gaol through an entrance tower with gates on the west side of Carliol Square.

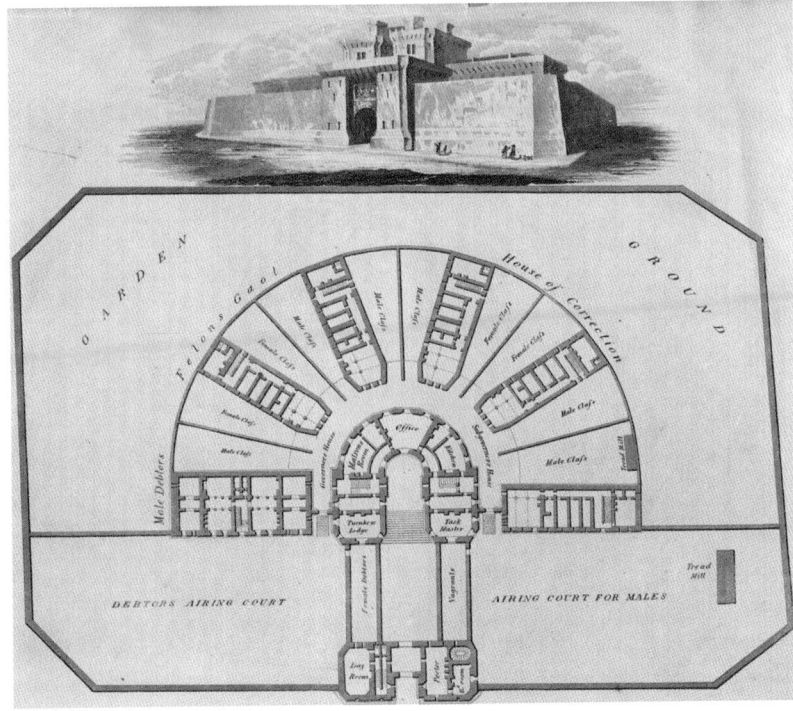

John Dobson's plan for the gaol.

Dobson produced a painting which shows how proud he was of this awe-inspiring feature which led to a grand staircase and another tower, a dramatic statement in stone and iron. Another interesting feature of Dobson's planning was that he consulted with 'more than one burglar of celebrity' to gain information on methods they used to escape prisons. This did not, however, prevent dozens of successful breakouts over the next 50 years.

John Dobson's painting of the Gaol, undated.

Dobson's plan was viewed by one admirer as 'a great and beneficent revolution in prison architecture' and a move away from the 'barbarous' era of manacles and fetters. The Gaol cost the enormous sum of £35,000 as Dobson was known to only use the finest materials in his constructions. High quality stone was sourced locally from the Church Quarry at Gateshead Fell. Indeed one local asked if they had built 'a palace or a prison?' Due to the high costs only five of the six radial wings were built and this meant that the Gaol was operating at capacity almost immediately after opening, a problem not helped by the fact that it housed debtors and felons.

The Gaol took almost five years to build and it opened to receive prisoners from the Moot Hall and Castle Garth in February 1828. The infrastructure was extensive and included wash-houses, store rooms, stables, work yards, a treadmill, and a chapel. The latter is interesting in that the system of classification which inspired Dobson's architecture was extended to church attendance. The historian Eneas Mackenzie described the arrangement for religious services:

'The semicircular part of the fourth story contains the chapel, which will be lighted from the sides of a dome. The prisoners will be marched from the upper gallery of their own wing, across an iron bridge, to the door of the chapel, which opens into their pew. There will be nine doors and nine pews for the different classes; and the pews being divided by partitions, extending to the roof of the chapel, the view of each class will be confined to the pulpit. The altar will stand in front of the pulpit, on one side of which will be a pew for the governor's family, and on the other one for the keeper of the house of correction. Behind this, and concealed by a screen, is space for another, which may be appropriated for female debtors. The clergyman, governor, &c. will have a clear view of all the congregation in their several boxes.'

This infrastructure required a great number of staff to manage the prisoners and the day-to-day operations in the Gaol. The Census of 1841 indicated that alongside the governor and deputy governor, the Gaol employed a porter, a turnkey, two taskmasters, warders and wardresses, a clerk, a matron, and several domestic servants. A surgeon and chaplain made daily visits to the prisoners and a schoolmaster and schoolmistress were added later. With this many staff and their families moving in and out of the grounds, it is clear that Newcastle Gaol was not only a space of punishment, but also a space for work, education, and reform. Although physically separated from the town by its walls, the inhabitants of the Gaol shared in the daily life and struggles of a growing urban centre.

Building the Gaol

On 4 June 1823 Mayor Robert Bell, in full regalia, led a procession of officials and commissioners uphill from the Guildhall to the plot on Carliol Croft where the new prison was to be built. Bell placed a glass vase containing contemporary coins in a cavity in the foundation stone. Over the stone was affixed a brass plate commemorating the event. Remarkably, these materials survived the demolition of the Gaol and over two hundred years later they are in the keeping of North East Museums. The Mayor then proceeded to lay the foundation stone with a silver trowel, which he later presented to Dobson, and addressed the concourse of persons assembled. He said,

'That he had then the honour of laying the foundation stone of a structure, which from the choice of its situation, and the rigid economy of the commissioners in its erection, would, he trusted, meet with the approbation of his fellow townsmen; the commissioners had, in determining upon the plan of the prison, anxiously consulted the preservation and improvement of the health and morals of those who might be confined in it; he did not add 'their comfort', because he saw no reason why criminals should enjoy comforts, which are beyond the reach of many honest and industrious persons.'

The Mayor concluded by expressing 'his fervent hope, that by the system of labour, which would be adopted in the prison, and by a strict attention to the morals of its inmates, those whose fate it might be to be placed in that prison, would return to society better men and better subjects than when they first entered its walls'. This address was received with nine hearty cheers from the crowd, and the completion of the ceremony was announced by the discharge of artillery from the Castle, and the ringing of the bells of several churches.

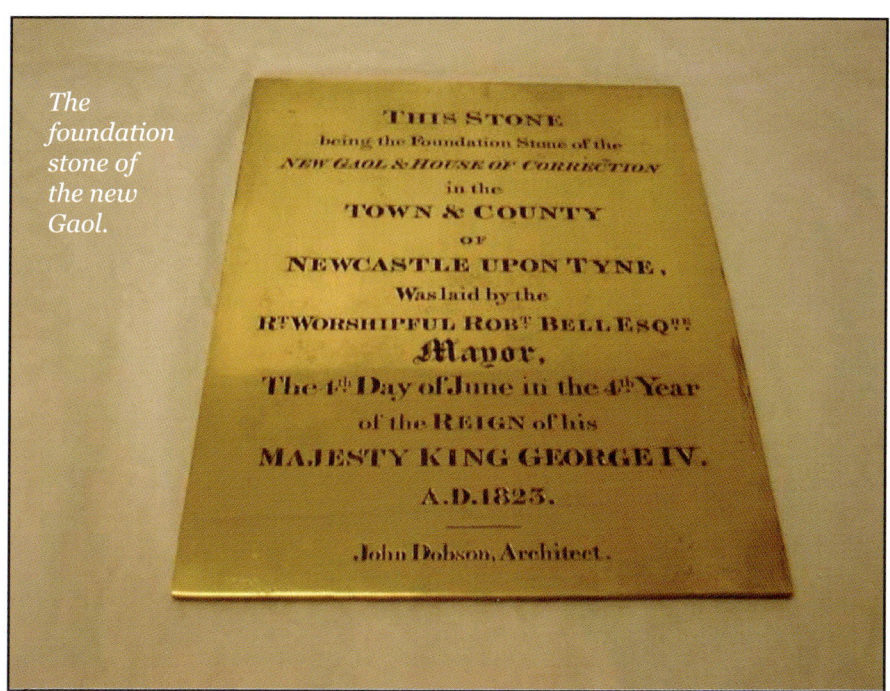

The foundation stone of the new Gaol.

The Operation of the Prison 1828 - 1925

Newcastle Gaol opened in 1828 to great optimism and confidence. It was hoped that the chaos and corruption of Newgate was in the past and that prisoners would now receive adequate means to work and receive instruction in a well-managed institution, and thereby be reformed. Alongside the new prisons being built in Britain came a new prison inspectorate run centrally by the Government to ensure standards were being met. Yet, despite the early promises, by 1838, when regular inspections of prisons commenced, Newcastle Gaol was condemned as unsuitable, damp, overcrowded, and lacking in pathways to reform. Prison reports indicate that cells were just 25 square feet [2.4 metres square] and most rooms were unheated. The Town Council minutes indicate that from 1836 there was a gradual laxity in prison discipline with alcohol circulating and regular fights. In the same year there were 176 prisoners incarcerated in a space designed for 100. Already there had been several escapes and an ingenious plot to make a set of keys from lead taken from water-closets. The prisons inspector complained that prisoners seemed to spend as much as 16 hours a day in bed during the winter months and the chief activity for the men was breaking stones and working the treadmill. Compounding the problems were the presence of debtors, who were typically incarcerated under different conditions from criminal offenders. In stark contrast to prisoners, debtors could have visitors for three hours per day and receive three pints of ale. They often sold the alcohol, and smuggled tobacco, to the other prisoners.

Prison inspectors continued to condemn Newcastle Gaol in the 1840s, recommending a complete rebuild, reform of labour projects, and the sacking of some staff. In the 1841 report the inspector complained about the 'gruffness' of some of the officers in their dealings with prisoners, but he was informed 'that a harsh mode of speech is common in this district, and that it does not indicate unkind feelings'. Another persistent criticism was that there was no proper classification system to manage the prisoners. It was only in 1840 that boys began to be separated from the men. The prison inspector noted that many of these boys were committed for petty thefts on the Quayside of old rope and scrap iron.

The number of arrests for such petty theft increased following the establishment of the River Tyne Police in 1845, and the Newcastle Borough Police were expanding in numbers and remit, contributing to more arrests and committals. Police force numbers rose steadily from 164 in 1869 to 200 in 1875 and to almost 300 in 1890. This increase in policing was matched by the rise in the daily average of inmate numbers, from 94 in 1838 to 182 in 1863 to 301 in 1909. In 1846 there were 99 prisoners present on the day of inspection: 14 were Scots, and 19 were Irish, reflecting the mixed roots of people in Newcastle. Of the 750 prisoners entering and leaving the Gaol in 1846, only four were registered as able to read and write, a finding which reflects the shocking statistics gathered at the time. Indeed, statistics indicated that out of a population of 51,000 in Newcastle, nearly 8,000 were children between the ages of five and 15 who were not in education. Many of the child prisoners in the Gaol - especially the Irish - were from Sandgate which was considered the most impoverished district of the town.

SANDGATE IN 1856

In 1856 an anonymous correspondent in the *Newcastle Journal* toured the alleys of Sandgate, describing in graphic detail his impressions of human 'pigsties'.

'In these confined alleys, where the sunbeams never enter, are closely packed together thousands of human beings in every stage of misery and wickedness. In the street you will never fail to see ruffianly looking men, whose acquaintance on a dark night is not by any means desirable. There also you may see women, brazen in face, foul of tongue, clothed in filthy rags, and squatted "on their hunkers" by the wayside. Everything wears a jaded and worn-out aspect - nothing flourishes but the taverns.'

Following condemnation from many quarters, Dobson was brought back over 30 years after the prison opened to redesign the accommodation. He replaced the five radial wings with three multi-story wards for men, women, and debtors.

Most of the prison population were young men and violence among prisoners was common which led to the need for strong discipline and punishment. In the 1850s some women prisoners were punished with cold shower baths and muzzles. Many prisoners took their own lives and the coroner was a regular visitor to the prison, investigating sudden or unexplained deaths. The Gaol also held women and children.

The location of the Gaol caused many problems for the authorities as it was situated east of Pilgrim Street - Newcastle's main street connecting the Quayside with the town. The pubs around Carliol Square were busy, especially on execution days. The already-busy district became more cramped in 1837 when the town's August fair moved to the streets around Carliol Square. Each summer, showmen arrived with performing monkeys, wild beast shows, roundabouts, swings, and fortune tellers - all a stone's throw from the Gaol. In 1864 the Governor told a Town Council meeting that the shouts and noises from the fair, which carried on until the early hours of the morning, caused disorder and disturbance among the inmates. In the 1850s it was common for inmates in the stone yard to toss rocks over the wall as a signal to friends outside to throw in contraband. Sometimes, rocks hit passers-by or damaged property on Carliol Square. Other disturbances came from beyond the prison walls. In 1859 Inspector Elliott of the Newcastle police intercepted a package thrown into the Gaol - it was addressed to a female prisoner and contained tobacco, liquorice, and a love letter.

Nevertheless, the Gaol was more than simply a place to house prisoners - it was community of sorts. The gates were opened many times each day to admit deliveries, visitors, workers, prisoners, policemen, and many others. It was also a home for the governor and deputy governor, and their families.

A major change in the history of the Gaol came in 1877 when it passed from the control of the Town Council and power was centralised in the hands of the newly established Prison Commission in England and Wales. Newcastle Gaol became known as Her Majesty's Prison Newcastle (HMP Newcastle) and the governance structure was shaken up. However, the old problems did not go away. Despite reforms, the number of inmates - reaching annual average figures of over 5000 by the 1890s - put the prison under increasing pressure. In 1895 a prison

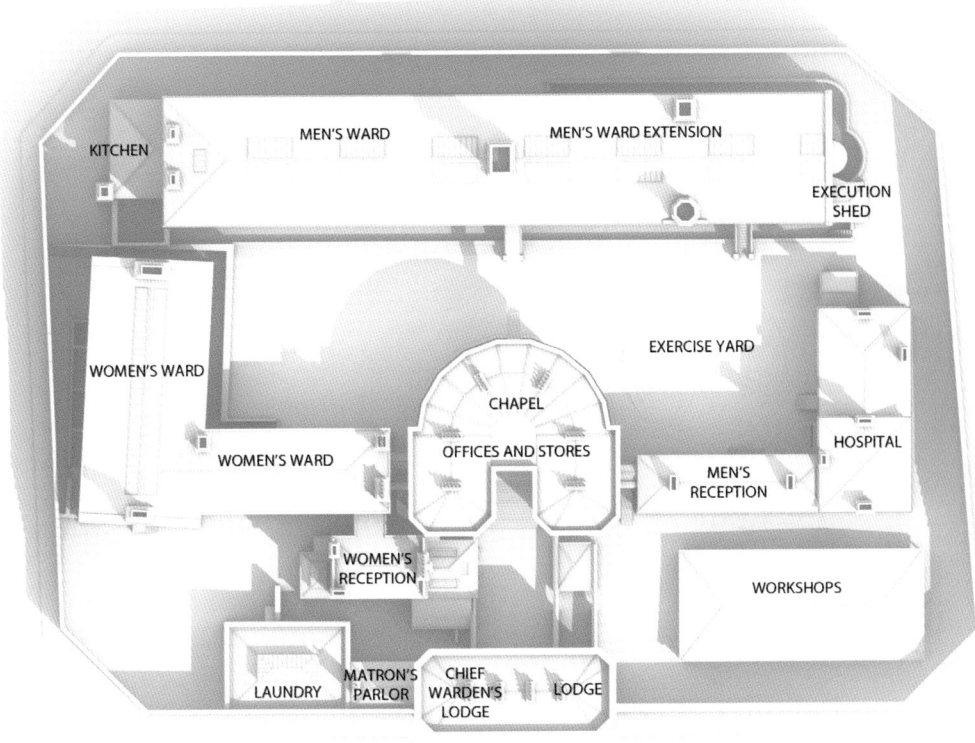

Reconstruction showing the late nineteenth century layout.

commissioner told a Parliamentary Committee meeting that 'Newcastle is the worst prison you have got'. The problem with the site of the prison, the condition and state of the buildings, and the failure to reform repeat offenders demonstrated that HMP Newcastle was not fit for purpose. From the late 1890s authorities began planning to demolish the failing prison but it took 30 years for the Home Office to act. In 1925 the prison was finally closed, the contents sold or destroyed, and the remaining prisoners transferred to HMP Durham.

What went wrong with a prison that had inspired such optimism in 1828? Certainly there was an increase in prison detentions associated with a growth in professional policing and the reduction of transportation as an option for judges in the mid nineteenth century. Another major issue was that the justice system still incarcerated debtors, which impacted on available space for criminal offenders - it was not until 1869 that major reform of debt legislation was passed. Fundamentally, however, this was a city centre prison responding to an increase in Newcastle's population, an increase in the policing and punishment of poverty-related crime, and the extensive growth and development of the urban fabric around its walls.

Visualising a Lost Prison

Newcastle Gaol dominated the East Pilgrim Street area between 1828 and 1925. Yet despite its historic presence in Carliol Square many people today are unaware that it existed. Interest was rekindled in the 1980s by Barry Redfern, a former police superintendent, who carried out pioneering historical research on the prison, including recording oral histories with former residents of Carliol Square.

However, widespread amnesia about Newcastle Prison remains, a situation not helped by the fact that there are few visual records. North East Museums preserves John Dobson's original plans but, aside from a few grainy black and white photographs and pencil sketches, this is all that remains of a visual record of the Prison. Fortunately, digital modelling and visualisations offer us a means to reconstruct this lost cultural heritage, placing the buildings in their correct context and bringing to light details that might otherwise have been overlooked.

As part of this book, the digital heritage company New Visions Heritage was commissioned to use Dobson's plans to digitally reconstruct images of the prison. Taking on the role of a detective with a limited number of clues, New Visions Heritage rediscovered forgotten aspects of the design of Newcastle Prison, details that traditional historical methods alone could not have uncovered. These visualisations offer a glimpse into parts of Newcastle Prison that have not been seen since its demolition in 1925 and help us to understand more about Newcastle Prison and how it operated in its near 100 year history. These exciting images are discussed later in this book.

Photograph of the exercise yard with a bridge leading from the cells to the chapel.

A reconstruction of the Prison's landings.

Conclusion

In 1856 a visitor to Newcastle Gaol praised the cleanliness and order of the system he found there. 'A vast deal of misplaced philanthropy', he wrote, 'is wasted upon the criminal population, and it certainly seems rather a singular anomaly in our boasted civilization that society should keep the people in pigsties till they become criminal, and then build palaces for them.' This chapter has covered some of the early history of Newcastle Gaol, including its concept and operation. But spaces of incarceration are about more than bricks and mortar. What about the lives of the prisoners within these dark walls? How did men, women and children survive and pass the time in the prison that Dobson designed?

In 1862, the *Newcastle Journal* captured the uneasy public perception of the Gaol:

'There are few places in Newcastle with which the general inhabitants of the town are so little acquainted as the dismal-looking pile of buildings occupying the centre of Carliol Square.'

Although the general population of Newcastle may have had little knowledge of the Gaol, it was far from being hidden or remote. The Gaol was a brooding presence, adjacent to Newcastle's bustling commercial heart. It was a place to be feared 'where none can thrive.' This reality was in stark contrast to the initial optimism surrounding its construction as a model of modernity, designed and built to the highest standards. An 1846 visitors' guide praised the Gaol's outward appearance and encouraged tourists to appreciate it as 'admirably well adapted to the improved system of prison discipline recommended by the philanthropic [John] Howard'. However, such praise was misplaced. Throughout its existence, the Gaol faced criticism from authorities and inspectors alike, condemned as unsanitary, unfit for purpose, and a breeding ground for crime - a den of thieves rather than a deterrent. Despite the lofty ambitions of its founders, Newcastle Gaol never achieved its promise of becoming a beacon for penal policy.

This chapter discusses life in the prison for the inmates, and offers an insight into what life would have been like for the men, women and children who found themselves deprived of their liberty within its walls during nearly a hundred years of changing regimes. Nineteenth century prisons were designed to be externally imposing and internally frightening. Local prisons, like Newcastle, were built close to the centre of towns, rather than outside civic boundaries, to act as a visual deterrent for those who contemplated breaking the law. The strategic placement was meant to serve as a reminder and a warning. What follows, discusses the working of the prison in selected periods of time, taken from accounts of those that experienced life inside. It includes details of daily life and discusses work, punishment, and the mundane by highlighting stories of some of the people who involuntarily walked through 'the gloomy and mysterious portal which separates the denizens of the gaol from the outer world.'

Penal Regimes

The treatment of inmates in the Gaol was influenced by many factors, including the strategy of each governor and, later, the direction of central government. Each new governor or national policy initiative had a direct impact on the daily lives of prisoners, who, once incarcerated, had little autonomy. Due to the different classes of prisoner and shifting regimes, it is impossible to set out a universal experience. However, snapshots of daily life offer valuable insights from which a good understanding of day-to-day life can be gleaned.

Postcard from 1910 showing where the prison sat within Newcastle.

Generally, as would be expected, life inside was hard. In 1858 a severely critical letter from the chaplain, John Irwin, laid bare some of the long-term failings of the Gaol. It was, said Irwin, a 'paradise of thieves', a 'nest of villainy', 'a hotbed of vice', and a 'house of corruption'. There was no heating or lighting; there were no useful tasks to employ the inmates; prisoners communicated with each other in contravention of the rules; huddled together, 'each corrupting the other.' In the same year, the inspector of prisons, Sir John Kincaid, reported that the Gaol was 'calculated rather to promote crime than to punish or to reform.'

Over the years, Newcastle Gaol implemented several penal systems in its quest for effective prisoner management and reform, such as the Silent System which enforced silence among prisoners to attempt to prevent the spread of criminal knowledge and encourage introspection and the Solitary System, borrowed from American models like that in force at Pentonville in London aimed for reform through isolation. An 1863 guidebook told its readers that 'the utmost order and quietness prevails within the walls'. Both systems were criticised for being punitive rather than productive and causing mental distress for inmates.

Prison regimes encouraged prisoners to be active and not idle. Prison work had a dual purpose of punishing and rehabilitating through labour. 'Work' was not necessarily productive or useful; as late as 1863 a report by a committee chaired by the Earl of Carnarvon advocated the treadmill and the crank as work, punishment, and a conduit for reform. The monotony of much of the 'work' was designed to encourage reflection and reform.

With a chapel at its core, the Gaol emphasised the importance of religious worship and, later, education as means of rehabilitation. Religious instruction included daily services and lectures to instil moral values and practical knowledge. The images opposite show the chapel at Lincoln Castle, and at Pentonville (opened in 1842). Pentonville operated under the Separate System, which was eventually introduced in Newcastle. Although there are no images of the interior of the Gaol in the early days, from the plans we can assume that the chapel at Newcastle was similar to these designs. Each Sunday the inmates attended at least one religious service. The services were not just spiritual events but offered opportunities for limited social interaction in an otherwise isolated environment. Sometimes special sermons were preached, for example in 1889 the Bishop of Newcastle gave a sermon on the consequences of sin, that lasted for 45 minutes; several men and women in the congregation wept bitterly throughout the service.

Examples of prison chapels at Lincoln Castle, top, and Pentonville, above.

The Prisoners

Newcastle Gaol housed several categories of prisoners, each with different requirements and subject to different punishments. Sentences served in a local prison, such as Newcastle, were short. The buildings in Carliol Square contained a gaol, a house of correction and a debtors' prison and held men, women and children. In the early days prisoners of both sexes and all ages were housed together but over time segregation became the norm. Some inmates had been convicted and were serving a sentence of punishment, and some were waiting to be tried. After conviction, prisoners sentenced to lengthy terms of imprisonment were initially held in the Gaol before being transferred to a convict prison, usually in the south of England or, in the early nineteenth century, to prison hulks, which served as a staging point for transportation to the colonies.

ELIZABETH BROWN

This story highlights a typical female inmate incarcerated in the Gaol: a poor woman, unable to pull herself out of poverty, regularly found drunk and often the victim of assault.

In January 1862 Elizabeth 'Bouncing Bess' Brown, alias Chambers 'a notorious character' aged 28, was found dead. Bess had led a sad life, and was a regular attender at the Police Court for drunkenness and brawling, and once for attempted suicide. She was in and out of the Gaol for petty offences and described as 'one of the most troublesome of the class of incorrigible offenders'. In 1860, she had promised to 'go straight' after one of the magistrates, Alderman Dodds, had scolded her: 'Why, woman, I see you have been here 42 times.' Despite Bess's best intentions, she did not 'keep out of trouble' and sadly ended her life, much of which had been spent in the Gaol, in a ward in the workhouse.

Punishment and Work

The management of prisoners through work and punishment was a key aspect of the Gaol's mission. Sometimes it is difficult to distinguish between tasks designed to be work and those that were purely for punishment. Work included stone breaking (sold for road building), sewing, oakum picking and mat making. Physical exercise meant that many prisoners became fit and strong.

The image below shows Cold Bath Fields House of Correction in London where the prisoners are picking oakum; sitting in silent rows, with their heads bent, this was hard, painful, work. Oakum picking involved unravelling tar-soaked ropes into loose fibres (oakum) which was then used for sealing the seams of wooden sailing ships. Oakum picking was a common task for prisoners in Newcastle, with one of the earliest documented references being in 1840. The image from Cold Bath Fields reflects what it would have been like in Newcastle where prisoners picked oakum in the yard. Oakum picking became a symbol of the harsh conditions of penal institutions, and the practice was gradually phased out as prison reform progressed in the nineteenth century.

Large oakum room (under 'Silent System').

In addition to work which was punishing, punishments for transgressions of rules could be meted out by warders. Discipline in the Gaol was generally good but if punishment was deemed necessary, it included corporal punishment (flogging), cold shower baths, restriction of diet and confinement in a dark or a light cell. Reports indicate that staff at Newcastle had less recourse to flogging than other similar prisons, preferring to use dark cells to punish disorder. A dark cell was a punishment cell where prisoners were confined in complete darkness and silence, often for several days. The only source of light came from a small hole in the door, used by guards to check on the prisoner. Many gaols in England and Wales used dark cells: there is an example that can still be visited in Beaumaris Gaol in Wales. Prisoners would not be let out for exercise during their time in the dark cell and were given a reduced diet of bread and water. There were no comforts: only a plank bed. Whether the point of sending prisoners for a period of confinement in darkened isolation was to punish, to allow the prisoner time to reflect upon their actions and to reform, or to temporarily remove a potential source of indiscipline, we do not know, but in the oppressive and overwhelming silence and the solitude it must have been easy to lose track of time and become disorientated. In 1855 the prison inspector compared the dark cell at Newcastle to a dungeon, 'worthy of the dark ages, and truly disgraceful to a civilised country'. Despite this criticism, Newcastle Gaol did not stop using it. Plans for alteration works in 1862 show four purpose-built dark cells which have no windows, and the entire section of cells could be closed off to cut out natural light. The punishment was eventually discontinued in the 1870s because of its cruelty and the severe mental and physical harm it inflicted on inmates.

Corporal punishment, although used sparingly at Newcastle, was a common disciplinary measure used to maintain order and punish inmates for misbehaviour. Typically carried out with a whip or a cat-o'-nine-tails, flogging was administered for offences such as insubordination, escape attempts, or failure to follow prison rules. The practice caused severe physical and psychological trauma. In 1844 six instances of corporal punishment were recorded in the Gaol. The lashes were inflicted using a rod, or birch, which was viewed as 'more civilised' than the cat o' nine tails. The writer of a letter to the *Newcastle Journal* recorded his horror at the use of the punishment saying, 'the rod is seldom inflicted, because almost everybody throughout the Empire is averse to the degrading method of flogging our own species.' Despite acknowledgement that the practice was barbaric, flogging was not abolished in English prisons until the Criminal Justice Act 1967, although the last recorded use was in 1962.

Flogging could be ordered by the court as an 'add-on' to a sentence of imprisonment, if the crime had been carried out with extreme violence. This additional punishment was not regularly ordered for prisoners held in Newcastle. A report to the government in 1864 listed the names of 12 men who had been birched, for offences such as stealing carrots and stealing iron, with the number of strokes ranging from 6 to 12.

A court case in 1869, described by the judge as 'the first case in this town in which the example had been made', led to Ralph Charlton, Thomas Charlton and William Fatkin being sentenced to 18 lashes (as opposed to being beaten with a rod). The punishment took place in the workroom of the Gaol in the presence of several magistrates, the mayor, the undersheriff, the governor, the prison surgeon and two doctors. The doctors were on hand to treat the men's lacerated backs. In 1872, when John Smith (alias Rochatt) was flogged, the viewers included reporters from several local newspapers who had been invited to witness the event. One journalist described the scene:

'the whipping post was erected in about the centre of the work shed and consisted of two stout uprights about 9 feet [2.7 metres] high placed firmly against the wall, and from the tops of these were brought in a slanting direction two pieces of timber of similar thickness. The back of the slanting portion of this framework was bordered about 6 feet [1.8 metres] up from the bottom, stout straps being affixed by staples at the bottom and near the top on each side. To this apparatus the wretched man was strapped… by his feet at the bottom and by his wrists high over his head. The instrument by which he was flogged was a regulation 'cat' having been expressly sent from the Home Office for this purpose. With the handle and lash together it was about two yards long, the lash being about a yard and a half and the handle about 18 inches long. The lash was composed of nine lengths of tightly twisted thick whipcord, each chord having hard knots tied in it near the end, while the extreme ends were carefully bound up with small thread to prevent their fraying out.'

Smith was lashed 18 times and suffered greatly. The punishment was described as 'a sickening sight' and caused many of those watching to feel faint.

The Whipping post and whip used at Wandsworth Gaol.

Daily Life

As a local prison, Newcastle Gaol was in the control of the town council until oversight was handed to the Home Office to ensure country-wide uniformity of discipline and diet, following the Prisons Act 1877. For most inmates, sentences were short and longer sentences were served in convict prisons far from family and friends.

Setting out a day in the life of a prisoner in Newcastle is not straightforward. A 'typical' day would be different for each class of prisoner. Political and military prisoners, suffragettes, German internees during World War I, and conscientious objectors would each have different tales to tell. And there is the official version - the plans for reform, cleanliness and education - in contrast to what actually took place. For example, prisoners were, in theory, provided with soap, but records show that it was not always available.

The Prison was not hermetically sealed and numerous people went in and out of the front gate each day. Some of the more unusual visitors included phrenologists, and the undertaker on the day before an execution, and the coroner following a death. The scant published eye-witness accounts from the prison describe hardship and brutality, as may be expected, but, on

One of the few surviving photographs of the Prison, c.1925.

THE NEWCASTLE CORONER

One infrequent, but important, visitor to the Gaol was the Newcastle coroner. The duty of a coroner was to hold an inquiry (an inquest), with a jury, in cases of sudden or unexplained deaths. Following the Capital Punishment (Amendment) Act 1868, the coroner was under a duty to hold an inquest on the executed.

Whenever an inmate died in the Gaol, the coroner would hold an inquest. During the lifetime of the gaol there were five coroners: William Stoker (1835-48); John George Stoker (1848-57); John Theodore Hoyle (1857-85); Theodore Hoyle (1885-1908) and Sir Alfred Appleby (1908-50, pictured).

occasion, compassion and kindness. The prisoners had access to a doctor who visited each day, and a medical ward for in-patient treatment. From the mid-nineteenth century there was education - the prison employed both a male and a female tutor. Accounts in the prison record books show payments for books purchased for the education of the inmates.

Prisoners spent much of their time inside their cells, except for short periods exercising or working in the stone-yard, garden, or kitchen, or attending a religious service. The prison design segregated male and female prisoners in different yards, and women were overseen by matrons and wardresses. Although governors assured inspectors that children were separated from older prisoners, concerns about offenders mixing together (raised as early as the 1820s) were reported in the 1920s.

Typically, a working day began at 5.45am when the prisoners

were woken by three chimes of a bell. Breakfast was served on a tin pan which was slid through the door by a warder who inquired if the prisoner was 'all right'. Bedding had to be folded, and the prisoner dressed for the day ahead. At 6am, tasks were assigned. Work continued until 7.30pm, 'dinner' was served at noon and 'supper' at 6pm. Prisoners who demonstrated good conduct could be assigned work in the kitchen. A school master provided instruction and monitored prison correspondence. Short periods of exercise in the yard punctuated the day. Even under a silent regime, exercise periods offered an opportunity to surreptitiously communicate with fellow prisoners. Within the tightly controlled regime, inmates used cunning to relieve the monotony of prison life; they schemed to claim extra food, talk to their compatriots through holes in the cell walls and smuggle tobacco. The cells were locked at 8pm.

On Saturdays the prisoners scrubbed and tidied their cells and were given a change of under-clothes. Shaving was forbidden, although barbers visited occasionally and some men managed to shave with sharpened knives. After the clean-up there was a rare period of leisure. Services on Sundays were held in the chapel. Meeting at the service provided a further chance to communicate with other prisoners under cover of the hymns and prayers. The service was led by a minister from the Church of England, with a Roman Catholic priest available for members of that faith.

The prison diet was intended to balance the health of the prisoner with punishment and discipline but it was intentionally meagre. In 1843 the government suggested that in local prisons, water and brown bread was enough for a 'fair state of health' and would avoid 'diseases which are commonly attributed to insufficient or improper diet.' Gruel, soup, and bread were the staples of the prisoners' diet, with cooked meat sometimes served depending on the dietary 'class' of the prisoner. Medical officers could prescribe more food, or different diets, on medical grounds. For example women prisoners with babies and young children, and women sentenced to hard labour could be given extended rations. Women and boys under the age of 14 were served less food than adult men and prisoners being disciplined were put on a punishment diet.

Visits

Prisoners were permitted to have limited visits from friends and family. Once every three months was the norm. As many inmates in Newcastle Gaol served terms much shorter than three months, some would receive no visitors during their time inside. In addition to a visitor every three months, the prisoner could write and receive one letter. Before 1862, prisoners and their visitors met on either side of the iron gate of the exercise yard. When the Gaol was renovated in 1862, 'visitors' apartments' were built. These were buildings with three compartments separated by wooden partitions: a prison warder stood in the central section, with the prisoner in the compartment to one side and the visitor in another compartment to his other side. Communication took place through two square windows in the walls of the central compartment. The prison officer could see and hear everything and would prevent any physical contact or anything passing between inmate and visitor.

Inmate Uniforms

The stereotypical image of a prisoner is of a man in a suit with arrows. Such uniforms were provided in some prisons. In Newcastle, the uniform was designed to be practical and hard wearing and may have been higher quality than the clothing the prisoners wore outside. In the early days the male prisoner's uniform was an olive green 'flushing' jacket, flannel waistcoat and canvas trousers with striped cotton shirt. The men wore woollen caps and wooden clogs with iron inserts on the sole. The simple jackets were made from heavy, coarse, and durable woollen fabric and resembled jackets worn by sailors and outdoor labourers. Women prisoners were given blue and white bed gowns, coloured cotton petticoats, blue flannel petticoats, cotton shifts, coloured cotton neckerchiefs and clogs (without iron bottoms).

This uniform evolved over time. In 1879 it comprised of a jacket, on which was worn a board with the prisoner's cell number, a waistcoat, braces, shirt, undershirt, drawers, pork-pie cap, shoes, stockings, and rough cloth white/brown trousers with a yellow and white stripe running down them monogrammed 'NG' (Newcastle Gaol).

Eye Witness Accounts

The Gaol in 1835

First person records of day-to-day life in Newcastle Gaol are scarce, but there is a fascinating snapshot from 1835 in an interview with a child inmate. This account is from information given to a commissioner tasked with reporting to Parliament for the Select Committee of the House of Lords on Gaols and Houses of Correction. Such accounts should be treated with caution due to the imbalance of power between the interviewer and the interviewee; however, they remain our primary source of 'eye-witness' testimony. The information is provided by an 11-year-old boy, Joseph Bruce, and corroborates contemporary reports from prison inspectors, revealing that the noble aims of the official prison regime were not being met. Joseph Bruce, along with his friend John Jones, aged 12, had stolen money from the Haymarket Hotel on Percy Street in central Newcastle in 1835. At the time of the interview, Joseph was imprisoned in Millbank Penitentiary in London, serving a two-year sentence before being transported to Australia. He recounted that he had spent one month in Newcastle Gaol prior to his transfer to Millbank.

Joseph's account gives an insight into the Gaol which then housed circa. 150 prisoners in 66 cells, with access to 13-day rooms. It was so overcrowded that it required the addition of approximately 48 cells to deal with the volume of prisoners. Despite the semi-panopticon design there seems to have been no identifiable penal regime. Neither the Separate System nor the Silent System were in force in Newcastle in 1835.

Joseph and John were described in the newspaper as 'urchins' but they were not hardened criminals. Joseph had previously been charged with stealing shoes (a common crime) but had been acquitted and John appears to have had no previous brushes with the law. Theft from houses or business premises was viewed as a serious crime and the theft with which they were charged was of high value: the boys had stolen a purse containing seven five-pound notes, four sovereigns, two half sovereigns and four pounds in silver. The young thieves, following the theft, did not escape far and officers from the new police force apprehended Joseph and John in the Shield Field, not far from the Quayside, where they were trying to destroy the paper money. The boys were taken to the police court. Their age did not afford them special treatment, and the magistrates sent them to Newcastle Gaol to await trial at the next assizes (the criminal court for serious offences). This image from Tothill Fields prison showing boys exercising in the prison yards gives a flavour of what John and Joseph would have faced in Newcastle.

Boys exercising at Tothill Fields Prison.

The debtors at Newcastle were held separately under different conditions and lived in relative comfort. They had a bed, fireplace, and access to natural light. Imprisonment did not absolve the debt, which resulted in prolonged incarceration for many. When Her Majesty's Inspector of Prisons visited the Gaol in 1850 he found a man of 81 years who had been in prison for six years and had become 'stone-blind.' Debtors could have visitors for three hours each day and received three pints of ale. There was a brisk trade in sales of this beer, and tobacco, to fellow prisoners. At Christmas the local great and good gave gifts to the debtors, for which a notice in the local newspapers was taken out to express their thanks. For example, in January 1838, the notice read 'The Debtors in Newcastle Gaol return their most sincere thanks for the kind donations they have received... they trust the public will still extend the hand of charity to the many sufferers still in Gaol: any small donation will be thankfully received.' The gifts that year included a fat sheep, from the Duke of Northumberland, and money from the mayor, the sheriff and a local Member of Parliament. In other years, a 'Christmas loaf', clothing and linen were sent as charitable gifts.

Sketch of a debtors cell.

measured, their religion recorded, and they were given prison clothing. A towel, comb, wooden spoon and soap were provided. Haircuts were ordered if the prisoner was particularly unkempt or had head lice.

The author was taken to his cell on the east side of the prison where there were cells for 250 male prisoners in four tiers. The women were housed parallel to the north wall. In the cell was a plank bed, a wash basin, table, stool, earth closet, tap with cold water, a tin pan, pint-pot and three large rugs. The cell had a bell to summon the warder. The cell was about 14 feet by 10 feet [4.3 metres by 3 metres] with a large 12 paned window. The prisoner's first meal was a piece of dry bread. After a month, the prisoner was given a more comfortable hammock bed - perhaps because of earning 'privileges' by being well-behaved. The prisoner explained that complaints about treatment could be made to the inspector of prisons for the Northern District who regularly attended the prison. Despite hardships, the author of the newspaper account believed the system was orderly, temperate, and capable of inspiring reformation.

Thus far we have discussed the lives of the convicts in Newcastle, however, from the opening of the Gaol until 1869 a separate class of inmates was incarcerated alongside the criminals. These were the debtors.

Debtors

During the 18th and early 19th centuries, individuals who failed to repay their debts could be confined to debtor's prisons, and Newcastle Gaol included a debtors' prison. The imprisonment of those who owed money played a significant role in the enforcement of debts. The practice was rooted in the idea that the fear of imprisonment would compel debtors, or their families, to settle outstanding obligations. Detainees were required to pay for their accommodation.

with light iron galleries. It was clean and neat and designed to hold 135 prisoners. It was silent. The prisoners were confined in their individual cells where they ate and slept, but were allowed out for exercise and chapel. They worked in their cells and the journalist saw prisoners making doormats and coconut matting. The cells had few comforts, but they were clean and white-washed and furnished with a chair, table, shelves, and a hammock with four rugs. There was no fireplace, although the cell was heated by a central heating system, and there was running water, a gas light, and a bell to summon the warder. The prisoner was provided with two tin mugs - one for water and the other for soup or tea; a salt cellar and a wooden spoon; a Bible and Prayer Book, a slate and pencil, and a scrubbing brush. The journalist left, content that the new prison buildings and regime was superior to the old and would be a credit to the town.

The Prison in 1879

In 1879, an unnamed prisoner gave a comprehensive interview to the *Newcastle Courant*, and his story is a fascinating insight into the Prison by 'One who has experienced it.' The anonymous author describes being sentenced at the Pilgrim Street Police Court 'by the great unpaid' (the magistrates), to six months hard labour for a crime he does not name but is likely a crime of dishonesty, such as theft. He was first held in a cell at the court with other prisoners, where they passed the time smoking a contraband pipe. At 7pm the writer was restrained with 'snips' (handcuffs) and marched to the Prison in convoy. A mob of small boys, 'unbonneted women', and 'roughs' accompanied the procession.

When the party reached the front gate, the accompanying police officer rang a bell which summoned the warder who admitted the new arrivals. Once inside, the prisoners entered a reception room where they stripped and were given a bath. The prison rules were on the wall for those that could read: 'strict silence; no communication with other prisoners; no bartering of provisions; work hard.' The men were examined for distinguishing marks,

Some changes were made. In 1846 the Prisons Inspector (while noting the poor construction of the building) reported that conditions had improved, and *Richardson's Guide to Newcastle* in the same year boasted that the prison was judged for the purposes of security, classification, inspection and employment equal if not superior to any in the kingdom.

The Gaol in 1854

In 1854, a temperance reporter was told the building was 'as full as it could hold'. The following year the (oddly named) *Report on English Prisons in the District of Scotland* recorded that the average daily number of prisoners confined in Newcastle was 190, with a total of 1609 over the course of the year (300 more than the preceding year). This was more than double the number of prisoners the gaol was designed to hold. The report detailed the punishments inflicted upon the inmates for various offences whilst in custody, including use of a dark cell, shower bath, muzzle or head piece. The main forms of activity were picking oakum, breaking stones, sewing and knitting - this work included making uniforms for prisoners both in Newcastle and sometimes for Durham Gaol. Prisoners spent most of their sentence inside their cells, apart from short periods in the exercise yard, breaking stones, gardening, or working in the kitchen.

A Visit in 1862

In 1862, a journalist from the *Newcastle Journal* visited the Gaol, seemingly without prior arrangement, and demanded a tour. He was admitted with the blessing of the governor, Thomas Robins. At the time, John Dobson had designed revisions to the buildings and new wings were being completed. The journalist was allowed to explore the site and report his impressions, which were favourable. He told his readers that the inside of the new building for male prisoners was a 'large oblong stone edifice, lit by innumerable small windows.' The building housed tiers of cells women were held for being common prostitutes. Health was poor and diarrhoea was endemic. The prisoners were idle and unwashed and the debtors spent their days smoking and drinking. Later, the inspector recommended that the male and female prisoners should be kept apart and that the separate system be introduced - this would have satisfied Joseph.

The Gaol in 1843

In 1843, the Gaol Committee of local magistrates sent a report to the Town Council setting out their concerns. Although the prison was a mere 15 years old and had been built to 'the best model in the kingdom', the cells were too small, unventilated and unheated. The prison was designed to hold 90 prisoners, including three in the infirmary, but the average number of inmates was up to 108 at any one time. There should have been cells for separate confinement, but no such cells were provided. This meant that the prison was acting contrary to the Gaol Act and the governor (Samuel Thompson) could be held accountable. It was noted that Newcastle was expensive to run in comparison with similar prisons elsewhere. A particular concern was the lack of facilities to hold prisoners who had decided to give evidence against their co-accused (turning Queen's evidence). The lack of separate cells meant their lives were endangered. The magistrates had no power to classify prisoners and there was growing alarm that children were imprisoned within the general prison population, and fear that many prisoners 'would come out worse than they went in.' There were plans and discussions around teaching trades within the prison: tailoring, joinery and shoemaking, but sentences were too short to facilitate proper training. However, despite recognising that the prison was not fit for purpose, there was a general understanding that if the prison was made too comfortable it would be seen as a 'house of refuge instead of [a] place of punishment' which would lead to it being over-run by those for whom life outside was difficult and brutal. The Council recommended remedial works to designate some cells for separate confinement, but this was a sticking plaster over a gaping wound.

Joseph told the commissioner that Newcastle prison was loud and violent with 'no Attempt to keep Silence … [and] swearing and bad Talk', and because there was no work or anything to help pass the time, it was a school of crime with 'Talk of what they [the prisoners] had done … [and] Instruction in Crime'. Joseph could not read and write but he said that Bibles and testaments were provided. Despite this, he said, 'Religion was laughed at' and he had been afraid. He told the inspector he would have preferred a separate and silent system away from violence and noise. It is interesting that Joseph knew about such systems. He spent his time during the day in a room with nine other people, some convicted and some waiting to be tried. Although the Gaol Act 1823 mandated that prisoners should be segregated by sex, men, women and children were often housed together during the day. At night, Joseph slept in his own cell. The diet, for a young boy, seems quite generous. Each day Joseph was given one pound of bread, one pint of soup, two pints of oatmeal gruel and milk. Joseph would have had a hard life outside of prison and the prison food was possibly more nutritious than he would have been given at home.

Joseph and John were tried at Newcastle Assizes in February 1835. They were found guilty of theft, but they had the good fortune to be sentenced by Judge Baron Alderson who believed, rather than simply punish, prison sentences should encourage rehabilitation. For larceny (theft of personal property) the law mandated that the sentence must be transportation for life. However, Baron Alderson found a way to work around this draconian punishment: he sentenced the boys to two years in a penitentiary (Millbank) but told them if they were well behaved, he would recommend mitigation of the transportation sentence after the satisfactory completion of the prison sentence. The boys were taken back to the Gaol to await transport to London, to the sound of the anguished cries of their families, gathered outside the courtroom.

Joseph's account of conditions accords with the prison inspector's report from the same time: it was overcrowded, frightening, and dirty. Most of the prisoners were vagrants and many of the

An Extraordinary Prisoner

In addition to the 'everyday' inmates, the Gaol sometimes housed prisoners who attracted press-coverage and interest from the wider community. Not surprisingly condemned prisoners were the focus of newspaper speculation and fevered reporting but there were other prisoners who also generated headlines. In 1872, one prisoner attracted wide attention: the Countess of Derwentwater. Amelia Matilda Mary Tudor Radclyffe (c.1831–1880), the 'Countess of Derwentwater', was a pretender to the estates of the Derwentwater family and her case was a cause celebre. She claimed to be the granddaughter of John Radclyffe, the only son of the third Earl of Derwentwater and demanded her right to hold the estates as the only direct heir. In 1868, she dramatically occupied the ruins of Dilston Castle, near Hexham, in the Tyne Valley, raising the Radclyffe flag, and displaying family portraits. Her story was eagerly followed in the press and she attracted a crowd of supporters.

The Countess was declared bankrupt in 1871 but she refused to cooperate with the bankruptcy process and, in 1872, she was thrown into Newcastle Gaol for contempt of court. Her supporters contended that her incarceration was illegal and campaigned to set her free. A bill addressed to the Queen included the following:

'Did Her Majesty in Council order the Countess of Derwentwater, a high-born lady, to be taken as a captive by violent hands, and incarcerate her person, ill, and suffering with bronchitis, and at once deprived of liberty and fresh air, within the confines of walls not erected for ladies of rank and truthful noble blood?'

Perhaps the Countess found it more comfortable than living in a tent in a ditch near her 'ancestral' home but, in any event, she spent nine months in Newcastle Gaol from where she published addresses to her supporters and railed against her predicament. She caught the imagination of the public and her eccentric activities kept her cause in the public eye until her death from bronchitis in 1880. After her death, her claim was found to be invalid and a biographer of the Radcliffe family has suggested that she was, in fact, a school teacher from Yorkshire.

The Countess of Derwentwater.

Later Years

Given the high number of recidivist offenders in the Gaol, several reforming initiatives were launched in later decades to provide education, training, and post-release guidance. A Discharged Prisoners Aid Society was formed in the 1880s while, by the 1900s, an active Visiting Committee had improved the state of the prison library and delivered regular lectures to the inmates. A report from 1908 indicated that a 'lady visitor', Mrs Bentham, took an interest in the education of female prisoners and delivered addresses on 'Fresh air', 'Health', 'Burns and Scalds', 'Care of children', and 'Try again'. In the same year juvenile male prisoners were lectured on 'Courage' and 'Manliness' by Colonel Coulson JP, and the Reverend Bernard East, vicar of St. Ann's Church, gave a lecture on the exploration of Antarctica.

In the early twentieth century Newcastle introduced a form of the new 'Borstal system', which was an attempt to reduce the number of juveniles returning to prison by providing a strict rota of training, labour, and other activities. All male juveniles with a sentence of under three months were given the Borstal treatment, described in positive terms by the chaplain: 'every capacity of the youthful offender is worked upon for his advantage - morally by a course of lectures on secular subjects periodically delivered by one and other officials and authorities; physically by daily drill and exercise, and generally by close observation and strict isolation from older offenders.'

FORCE FEEDING IN WORLD WAR I

In World War I, men aged between 18 and 41, unless in an exempted category, were required to perform military service. Men who objected to fighting on moral grounds could apply to be granted an exemption. If the application for exemption was refused, the conscientious objector would be conscripted. Around 6000 men resisted conscription and were court marshalled and sent to prison for 112 days with hard labour with a mandatory minimum of one month's solitary confinement. Conscientious objectors described the Newcastle Prison as 'vast, friendless and impersonal'. One said that 'It was a very old prison, and it was terribly dark. Horrible little, tiny windows and everything. It was a wicked old prison'. Several conscientious objectors went on hunger strike in protest at the conditions. These men were force-fed and while their plight is less well-known than that of suffragettes, their stories of being force fed are just as harrowing.

Conclusion

Throughout its lifetime Newcastle struggled to cope with and provide suitable accommodation for the inmates in its care. It never had sufficient capacity for the numbers of prisoners sent to be punished or held before disposal elsewhere. Conditions in the prison were rarely ideal, although many of the inhabitants may have found running water, heat and a dry place to sleep with basic food, more appealing than their lives outside of prison.

In the next chapter you will meet some of the staff and find out about the people required to keep the Prison running.

CHAPTER 3

PRISON STAFF

On Tuesday 31 March 1925, the imminent closure of Newcastle Prison was commemorated in this newspaper photograph, of 'Newcastle Prison Officials.' The caption named some of the staff in the photograph: from left to right (seated): Mr F Carr (Clerk); Miss Ferguson (Matron); Major the Hon GE French, DSO (Governor); Rev JJ Pigg (Chaplain); Mr CB Lassey (Clerk). Standing behind the Governor was Chief Officer AH Todkill, and (inset) was Principal Officer J Stoves.

Behind stood unnamed prison officials, male warders wearing caps and uniforms, female warders in white bonnets. The photograph gives a sense of the community required to operate the prison. And this had been the case since the early days of the Gaol. In 1839, the prison staff consisted of the Governor, a Chaplain, Surgeon, Taskmaster, Matron, Principal Turnkey, Assistant Turnkey, Under Taskmaster, Assistant Matron, and Porter (listed in order of seniority). Until its closure in 1925, each decade the number of staff increased considerably, as the prison expanded. This chapter looks at some of the staff who worked at the Prison, their roles and some stories of the men and women who kept the prison operating.

A photo of the prison staff in the Illustrated Chronicle from 31 March, 1925.

Governor

As shown on the plan, the governor of Newcastle Gaol was intentionally and literally at the centre of the institution. His accommodation was the point around which the daily life of the Gaol revolved. Governors (and their deputies) lived inside the prison, usually with their families and household (including domestic servants). They were expected to always be available for prison duties and bore great responsibilities for the gaol, its staff and the prisoners. Their choice of regime shaped the prison experience, especially before prisons were nationalised in 1877. After that date, the duties of the governor were more settled and every morning they would visit each cell, to decide on any punishments for reports of misbehaviour, and inquire into any complaints made by prisoners.

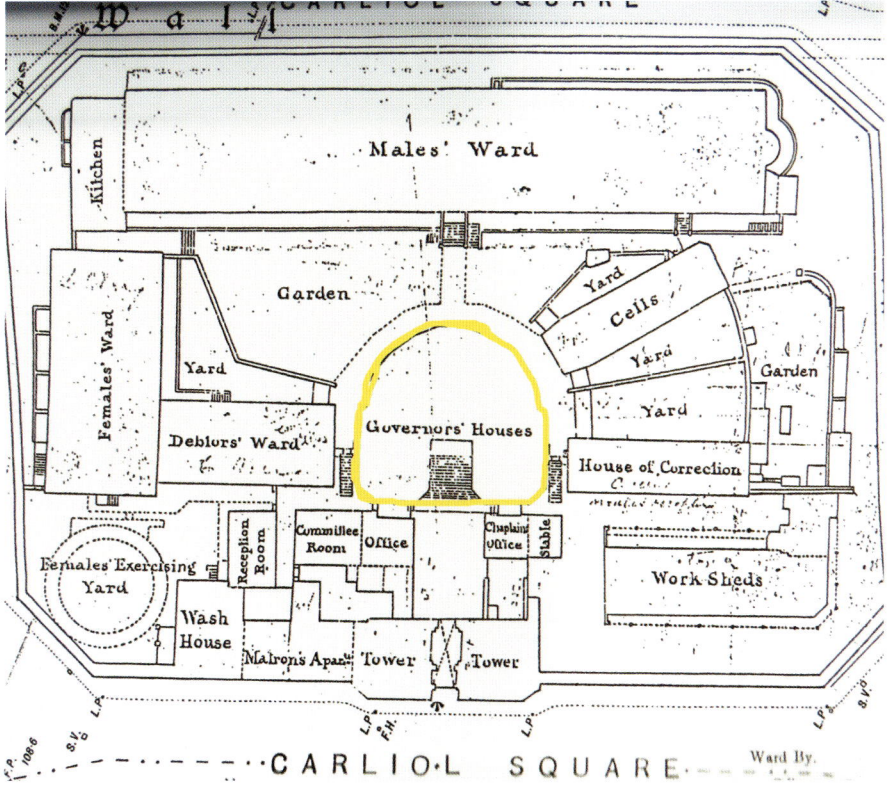

Plan highlighting the position of the Governor's house.

The governor of Newcastle Prison when it closed – shown in the photograph (as with all governors he did not wear a uniform) - was Edward Gerald French, son of John French, 1st Earl of Ypres. Educated at Wellington College in Berkshire, French fought in World War I. He was gassed and wounded in 1917, and mentioned in dispatches twice, being awarded the Distinguished Service Order (DSO). He had a varied career. He was deputy governor of Dartmoor Prison 1921-23 and made his first-class cricket debut for the Marylebone Cricket Club against Scotland in 1922. He was Commandant of the Bahamas Police Force in 1923 before becoming the last governor of Newcastle Prison in 1924-25.

The prison service offered good prospects for senior officials. This can be seen in the career of Henry John Hellier, governor of Newcastle Prison 1910-15. Hellier was born in Kent, the son of a clerk in the prison service. He joined the convict prison at Millbank as a Clerk, 2nd Class, in July 1878, aged 22, and worked in Wormwood Scrubs, Wandsworth and Lincoln prisons, before becoming governor at Dorchester Prison in 1899. He was then governor at Leeds Prison from 1908 before transferring to Newcastle in 1910, on an annual salary of £370. He governed at Newcastle for five years and was described in the *Newcastle Journal* as 'a painstaking and courteous official', who took 'a good deal of interest in the work of the Discharged Prisoners' Aid Society.' Hellier oversaw the executions in 1910, of John Alexander Dickman, and of John Vickers Amos in 1913. Hellier left HMP Newcastle in 1915, to become governor of Durham Prison.

Not all ex-governors left Newcastle for better things. In March 1830, Gilbert Grey was elected by Newcastle Town Council to be governor of Newcastle Gaol. Grey had been swordbearer to the Corporation of Newcastle since 1815, but even so the vote was tight: 13 votes for Grey, 12 for the other candidate. Those with doubts were proved correct because by August 1836 the Council had resolved to remove Grey as governor. An investigation by the visiting justices had 'left no doubt of the truth of the charges brought forward, that great neglect existed, and that the discipline of the prison had got into a very bad state, so much so, that it was necessary to appoint a new gaoler.' Worse was to come for Grey. Later that year he lost his claim for compensation for loss of office and in October 1838 he was declared an 'insolvent debtor'. Grey faced the possibility of being sent to the Debtors' Prison – inside the same walls where he had been governor.

One of the longest-serving governors of the Gaol was Thomas Robins, governor from 1860 to 1880. It was his first post in charge of a prison; previously Robins had been deputy governor of the Leeds Borough Gaol and House of Correction. We can get a good impression of life under the regime of Robins from the newspaper article written in 1879 by a former inmate of Newcastle Prison, sentenced in 1878 to six months imprisonment with hard labour.

SWORDBEARER

The role of swordbearer in Newcastle dates back to 1391, when King Richard II granted the mayor of Newcastle and all his successors the right to have a sword borne before them. By the 1820s the swordbearer was paid £55 a year. It was a ceremonial role – he accompanied the mayor on official occasions. The civic insignia of Newcastle today include two swords carried by swordbearers. One dates from around 1450, with a blade 34 inches (86cm) long. The newer sword dates from the late 1700s and is 54 inches (about 137cm) long. There is also the 'Cap of Maintenance', the official headgear of the Swordbearer, which is made of grey squirrel fur with a crown of crimson velvet and long gold cords ending in tassels. It is the same style as the swordbearer would have worn in 1391.

By that time, the prison had been governed by Robins for many years. The regime under Robins was harsh. He enforced strict silence and a meagre diet, saying 'I have no sympathy with those who would make a prison anything but a disagreeable place.' In 1863-4, 12 boys aged 10-13 convicted of offences of theft (including stealing apples, carrots, slippers or a sack) received between six and 12 lashes with a birch. Present on each occasion were Robins, Joseph Little, the deputy governor (described by the former inmate as 'another old and zealous official'), a warder, and Dr Nicholas Hardcastle, the prison surgeon. When Robins retired in 1880, the Mayor described him as 'a most humane man, and an excellent disciplinarian.'

Over time, increased prison inspections and national regulations led to general improvement in the calibre and performance of prison governors.

GOVERNOR MAJOR NELSON

Newcastle's inmates were unlucky to experience the regime of Governor Major James Osmond Nelson for only a short time in 1899. Nelson joined the prison service after a military career. Before Newcastle, he was governor of Reading Gaol from 1896 – 1899, including when Oscar Wilde was a prisoner there. Reading's previous governor used frequent and severe punishments, but Nelson showed Wilde kindness and allowed him to write, including *De Profundis*, one of Wilde's great works. Of Nelson and his impact as governor on the life of the inmates, Wilde wrote: 'though he cannot alter the rules of the prison system, he has altered the spirit in which they used to be carried out under his predecessor... he has quite altered the whole tone of the prison life.' Governor Nelson was known as 'a man of gentle and humane character greatly liked and respected by all the prisoners.' Sadly, he died in 1914, aged only 55.

Deputy Governor

Next in terms of seniority in the prison staff was the deputy governor. His accommodation was in the Gaol, with, 'a bright and cheerful apartment [office]' on the ground floor, according to a report of a visit by the *Newcastle Journal* in 1862. The journalists noted that the deputy governor kept a register recording the names and descriptions of the inmates, as well as the clock 'by means of which the slightest irregularity on the part of the warders who guard the interior and the exterior of the building may be detected.'

At times the deputy governor was responsible for securing each cell door at night, although this may have depended on the numbers of inmates and prison staff. Even when this was delegated to an under warder or the turnkey, the deputy governor could still bear responsibility for securing the prisoners, as in 1860 when the deputy governor, Wood, was suspended after the escape of three prisoners, including the notorious Walter Scott Douglas.

The position of deputy governor was often a step towards the role of governor. Several governors of Newcastle Gaol had previously worked as deputy governors elsewhere, including Thomas Robins and Edward Gerald French. Many had a similar military background, which might have been an advantage in the selection process.

Chaplain

While the governor was in overall charge of the prison, directing and deciding the day-to-day needs of prisoners and staff, the spiritual wellbeing of the prisoners was overseen by a dedicated prison chaplain.

At times this division could lead to tensions between the chaplain and governor. When the Gaol opened the chaplain had a separate room to meet with inmates, but in 1839 this was discontinued. In 1846 the then chaplain – the Reverend Lewis Paige – proposed that a new chaplain's room should be built in the debtor's airing (exercise) yard, but the Town Council refused to cover the £120 cost. In 1849 Reverend Paige asked instead for a room to be furnished for his use. The Town Council discussed allocating the necessary £25, on the grounds that 'as it was known that the chaplain and the governor [Samuel Thompson] did not agree it would be best to separate them, and keep them at peace.' To no avail: the chaplain did not get his own room and Reverend Paige resigned in 1852, after nine years at Newcastle Gaol. A dedicated office for the chaplain was reinstated later in the nineteenth century.

Chaplains played an often-overlooked role in the life of the prison and, more than most warders or governors, were usually the closest confidantes of the men and women serving their sentence. Religious observance to seek to rehabilitate prisoners, or to encourage them to reflect on their crimes, was an important facet of Victorian penal regimes. Alongside the governor's quarters, the prison chapel formed part of the centre of the Gaol and inmates were expected to attend Church of England services regularly, including on Sundays and for religious festivals. Services for other faiths were also permitted, with the consent of the governor; for example, a Roman Catholic clergyman could attend on Sundays.

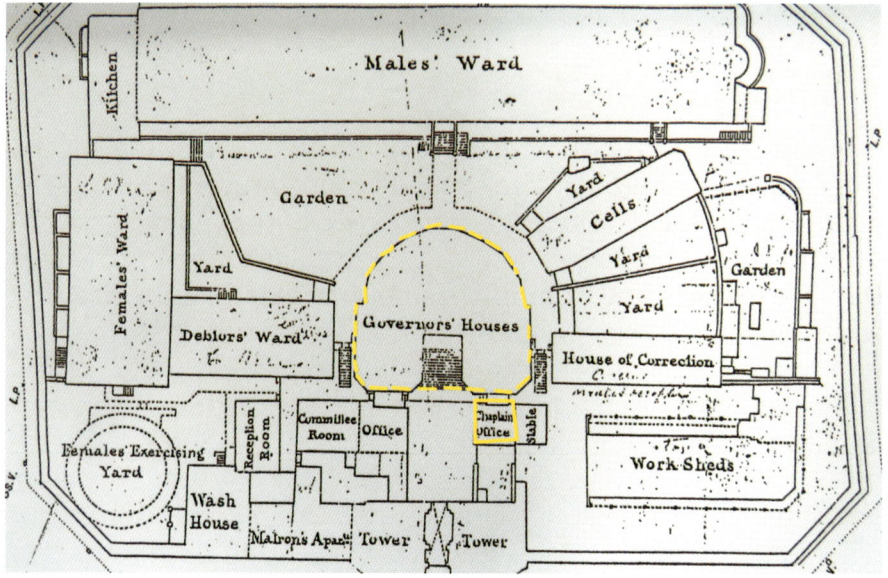

Location of the Chapel, in the same building as the Governor's House.

In the early days of the Gaol being a prison chaplain was not a full-time role. Many chaplains were vicars in the Church of England and carried on their work outside the gaol. However, in 1836 the visiting justices recommended that the chaplain should devote more of his time to the duties of his prison office, because 'the present religious services are not sufficient to reform men intimate with crime and ignorant of religious observation.' They recommended that prayers should be read every morning by the chaplain, not the gaoler, and that the chaplain should devote 'greater attention to the religious instruction of the younger prisoners.' They noted a recommendation that in prisons holding fifty or more inmates the chaplain should be 'required to devote his whole time to the prison, and should have no parochial duty to perform.'

When the Reverend Rayson Mandell was appointed chaplain in 1836, the salary was raised from £80 to £100 per annum because he was not permitted to hold any other clerical appointment with parochial duties. The chaplain's salary remained at this level until December 1844 when the Town Council considered increasing it to £150, 'in consequence of the great increase of [the prison chaplain's duties], arising out of the new prison regulations, and the advancing number of criminals.' By 1869 an advertisement for a new chaplain at Newcastle Gaol offered a salary of £200 per annum. In 1877 prisons were nationalised and the decision on salaries was taken out of town council control.

From the official report into the Gaol in 1839, the duties of the chaplain seem onerous: 'The chaplain reads prayers every day at 9am. He performs Divine Service twice on Sundays, with a sermon in the morning, and also Good Friday and on Christmas Day. He exhorts and admonishes the hardened and refractory, and attends to the spiritual wants of all the prisoners who require his assistance; he also distributes Bibles and Testaments, and other books of a religious and moral tendency from the prison library, to all who can read.'

The chaplain would also supervise a schoolmaster and schoolmistress employed to teach the inmates to read and write.

In addition, he kept a prisoners' character book and met regularly with prisoners. Although he was expected to visit all prisoners in their cells, the short sentences served by many inmates of local prisons like Newcastle meant that some would never see the chaplain. A chaplain would make special efforts to visit prisoners who were sick, or receiving punishment, and juvenile prisoners. In 1865, the prison chaplain Reverend Robert Sheppard had to counsel a woman charged with attempted suicide (then a criminal offence) while she was held in the Gaol for one week on remand before her trial, to bring her 'to a proper feeling in regard to her improper conduct.'

One of the most important and difficult duties of the chaplain was to support those in the condemned cell awaiting execution and to accompany them to the scaffold. In August 1844, the chaplain, Reverend Lewis Paige, had to minister to Mark Sherwood, executed for the murder of his wife. At the scaffold, on the Town Moor, Paige seized Sherwood's arm and said 'farewell' three times before reciting the Lord's prayer 'in a firm and elevated tone', becoming 'more impressive in his delivery, holding the culprit by the hand, and being apparently much affected.'

The Reverend William Faithfull Lumley was chaplain for nearly 25 years, from 1889. In that time, he worked with eight governors and attended six executions. In one case, that of Samuel Emery, a young soldier hanged in December 1894 for the murder of his former lover Mary Ann Marshall, Lumley wrote to the governor following a discussion he had had with the prisoner. Lumley believed that statements Emery made to him privately indicated the possibility of a plea of temporary insanity, which could have saved him from being executed had the Home Secretary accepted a plea for mercy. Despite Lumley's intervention, Emery was executed within the walls of the Prison in December 1894. The importance of the prison chaplain in these circumstances is clear from a newspaper report that Emery's last words were addressed to Lumley. The last execution that Lumley would see was that of John Vickers Amos in 1913, convicted of a triple murder, including two police officers.

REV. WILLIAM FAITHFULL LUMLEY

The Rev. Lumley may have sought relief from the sometimes-sad realities of his role as prison chaplain through his hobby (or near-obsession) of pigeon fancying. He became a leading authority on pigeons and specialist breeds. However, the highly competitive world of pigeon fancying could lead to heated arguments and in the case of Lumley, almost to jail. In June 1898, he was charged with assaulting a fellow competitor, a prison officer at Wandsworth County Gaol. Lumley's claim that his hand involuntarily struck the complainant on the nose was doubted, but, fortunately for Lumley, the charges were dropped. One report on his impending retirement from Newcastle Prison carried a photograph of Lumley, with his flowing white beard, captioned, 'Well-known bird (not gaol bird) fancier.'

Lumley also took a keen interest in the Prisoners Aid Society; many newspaper reports mentioned his good deeds to ex-offenders. The role at Newcastle was Lumley's last ministry; he retired from the clergy in 1914. However some chaplains left Newcastle to move to other gaols. The final two chaplains at the Prison, the Reverend HJ Donaldson Selby (chaplain 1921-24) and Reverend JJ Pigg (1924-25, the last chaplain at Newcastle (shown in the photograph at the beginning of this chapter, seated in the front row), both left to take up the chaplaincy at Durham prison.

Prison Surgeon/Medical Officers

Whilst the spiritual welfare of prisoners was administered to by the chaplain, their physical welfare was overseen by a prison surgeon. Newcastle Gaol had six surgeons in its lifetime. Two of the surgeons were followed in the role by their sons. The prison surgeon did not live inside the Gaol, and most of the men who held the post also ran a private medical practice. For example, Dr Thomas Michael Greenhow, prison surgeon in 1839-60, was senior surgeon to the Newcastle Infirmary from 1845 and Dr Nicholas Hardcastle was also medical officer at the Union Workhouse in Newcastle.

DR NICHOLAS HARDCASTLE

Dr Nicholas Hardcastle featured in an episode of the BBC's *A House Through Time*, presented by historian David Olusoga, as a former resident of 5 Ravensworth Terrace, Newcastle. Hardcastle was surgeon at the Gaol from 1860-1900. He was appointed despite criticism of his failure to properly treat children with 'the itch' (scabies) in his role as the medical officer at Newcastle Union Workhouse from 1854-1887. Cleared of misconduct, Hardcastle was free to take up the position of Gaol Surgeon and continue with his private medical practice. Later, more seriously, criticism of his treatment of an outbreak of scarlet fever at the Workhouse led to him being found guilty of neglecting his patients in 1887. Hardcastle resigned as the medical officer at the Workhouse but remained as surgeon at the Prison until 1900, when his son, Dr William Hardcastle, took over the role.

Prison medical officers had to balance their duties of protecting the inmates' health with enforcing prison discipline. What must have made the role particularly difficult was that most inmates served short sentences, so contact between doctor and inmate might have been minimal. The surgeon was responsible for the general health of the prisoners, their cleanliness and, perhaps more surprisingly, the preparation and quality of the food. In 1839 the official report into the Gaol noted that,

'The surgeon visits the prison daily, and sees every prisoner confined therein twice a week. He examines every prisoner brought into the prison. He enters the name of every sick prisoner in his journal, with the nature of his complaint, disease and the medical treatment.'

This was an onerous commitment and the report of a visit to the Gaol by the *Newcastle Journal* in 1862 referred to the surgeon making bi-weekly inspections of the inmates, which consisted of visiting each inmate in their cell and asking, 'All right?'. Often prisoners needing medical attention would notify the turnkey or the governor who would tell the surgeon at his next visit or send for him to come to the Gaol in urgent cases.

Some inmates would have had complex medical conditions; many would have been suffering from the effects of disease, poverty, and alcohol dependency. Inmates' general health would be affected by the prison regime and infectious diseases presented huge problems. While the prison diet was intentionally meagre, the medical officer could decide certain inmates needed a different diet; for example, nursing mothers, or prisoners sentenced to hard labour. The surgeon had to assess which inmates could carry out hard labour or face physical punishment. Dr Nicholas Hardcastle was present at the flogging of three men in 1869. The prison surgeon also attended executions. Their role was to confirm that death had occurred and to provide the necessary certification required by law. He would advise on punishment diets. Dr William Hardcastle, son of Nicholas Hardcastle, prison surgeon 1900-24, presided over the force feeding of suffragettes, and male prisoners who were imprisoned as Conscientious Objectors in World War I.

Schoolmaster and Schoolmistress

Education of inmates became increasingly important during the lifetime of the Prison. The photograph of the prison staff in 1925 made no reference to a schoolmaster or mistress, but this might not be surprising. In addition to being the schoolmaster or mistress, staff would likely have another role within the Prison.

The importance of education in prisons was recognised early, but the time and attention given to it depended on the approach of the governor. The standard of education available was also questionable: in the early years, turnkeys or warders might have had responsibility for teaching inmates to read and write. In 1835 it was recommended (but not then required) that every prison with more than 50 inmates should appoint a schoolmaster who was not one of the prisoners. (This suggests that in many prisons, it was prisoners who were attempting to educate each other.) In 1839 the official report into Newcastle Gaol noted that the position of schoolmaster was vacant. It might have been difficult to recruit anyone to take the job, because a year later in November 1840 Governor Samuel Thompson advertised in newspapers for a new schoolmaster to teach the Juvenile Prisoners 'Reading, Writing, and Arithmetic, and also some Mechanical or Handicraft Employment at intervals.' The salary was £50 a year. No indication was given of the qualifications required for this role.

The report of a visit to the Gaol by the *Newcastle Journal* in 1862 noted that the male wing had a small schoolroom, 'in which such prisoners as desire it can have an hour's instruction every day'. In 1879 the schoolmaster was Robert Smith, who gave male inmates 'elementary instruction to those who require it', as well as looking after the correspondence of prisoners, and distributing books from the prison library (roles previously performed by the prison chaplain). When prisons were nationalised in 1877 regulations for the education of prisoners were introduced which applied to all local prisons, but staff roles could still be combined. Education of prisoners was often delegated to the chaplain and Clerk and Schoolmaster (C&S) warders. In 1901, Isabella MacIntyre was both schoolmistress and prison warder.

Matron

The most senior woman in the Prison was the matron. In 1925, the matron was Miss Ferguson. The role of the matron was complicated: she bore the same responsibilities for the prisoners in her care as the governor, but without his authority, status and salary. She was responsible for the women's wing and female exercise yard; and she monitored when female prisoners went to chapel, not least to avoid any contact with the male prisoners. The matron's duties were set out in the Gaol Regulations and Additional Rules (1830) shown below.

The duties of the Matron in 1830.

The matron had to live within the prison walls. (Her accommodation within the Gaol is marked on the plan). That accommodation was provided may have made the role attractive, although the living quarters were above the laundry and were reported as being unpleasantly damp and warm.

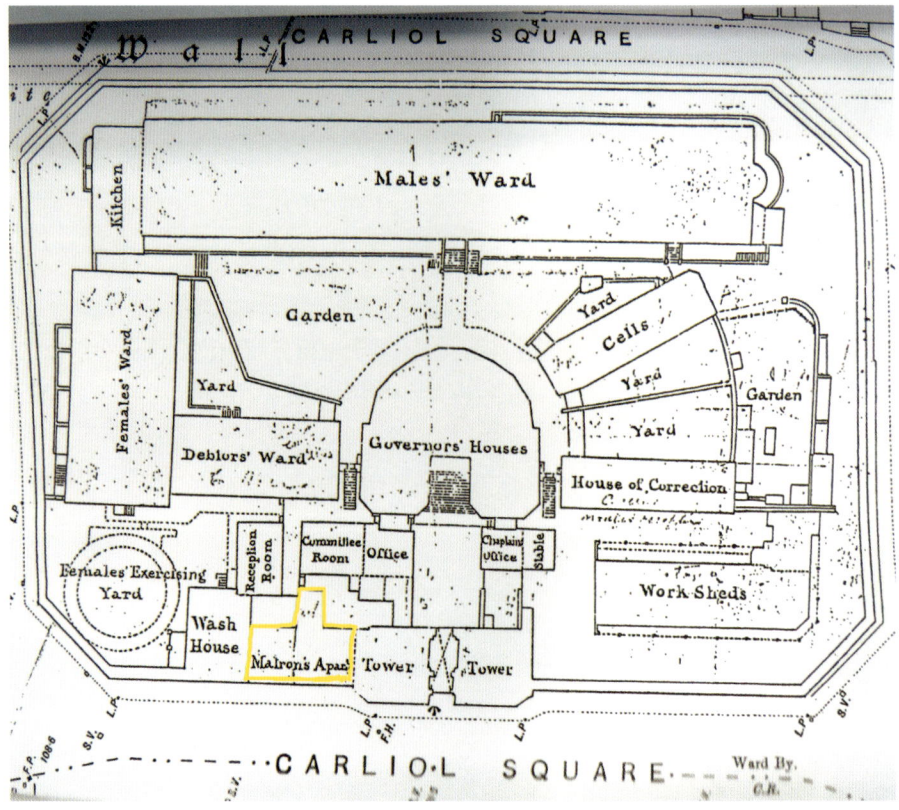

Plan showing the location of the Matron's house.

There was a steady turnover of matrons at Newcastle Gaol. In 1834, the office of matron was vacant and an application with 'an excellent character' (a reference) was received from Catherine Armstrong, a widow with four children, who lived 300 miles away, in Kent. Catherine had an unusual history. Born in 1792, in New Brunswick, she lived in Nova Scotia, Canada, and was the grand niece of the famous poet Oliver Goldsmith. In 1814, in Quebec, she married a sea captain from Wallsend, William Askew

Armstrong. The family moved to Kent, probably for William's career. Sadly, he died at sea in 1825. In 1834, Catherine Armstrong became matron at Newcastle Gaol and moved into the accommodation with her son (William, aged about 17) and daughter (Mary, aged about 12). It would prove to be a bad move for Catherine and her family.

Matrons had sole charge of the prison storeroom and its contents, including bedding for the inmates. In March 1835 a mattress or 'bed-tick' went missing from the storeroom. Catherine was charged with theft and was tried in Newcastle on 8 April 1835 - the same day that her son William also faced trial, charged with theft from his employer. William was acquitted by the jury, but Catherine's outcome was not so good. The court heard that the bed-tick was 'pawned by her daughter' Mary, and pawnbrokers' tickets were found in Catherine's room. Found guilty by the jury, the judge said that Catherine had violated the trust placed in her, made worse by using her daughter to dispose of the stolen property; he sentenced Catherine to be transported for seven years. According to the *Newcastle Journal*,

'a scene then took place which baffles description. The daughter shrieked and clung to the prisoner, who fell down at the bar, and the son, who had just been acquitted upon a charge of felony, fainted.'

Catherine was transported to Van Diemen's Land (Tasmania) in 1835. At the end of her 7-year sentence she chose to settle in Australia, and her surviving children joined her there.

In April 1836 Newcastle advertised for a new matron for the Gaol & House of Correction, with a clear specification: 'An active middle-aged woman of respectable character is wanted as matron in the gaol and house of correction at Newcastle-upon-Tyne. Salary, thirty pounds a year, with a house, coals, candles, and washing. A woman unencumbered with a family will be preferred.' Perhaps this last sentence was a tacit admission that Catherine's difficulties might have stemmed from a need to support her children.

The matron was assisted by a deputy matron and female warders. An advertisement for a new Assistant Matron in the *Newcastle Journal* in September 1837, asked for 'an active middle-aged Woman', offering a salary of £25 per annum, but only an allowance of £5 per year instead of the house, coals, candles and washing provided for the matron. Perhaps the position was difficult to fill; it was not until January 1838 that a Mrs Rudd was appointed.

The role of matron could be a dangerous one. Like the male staff, the matron could face violence from inmates - even in the Women's Wing. In 1878, a woman named Ann Docherty, aged 24, was held in Newcastle Prison, and a note on her file reads: 'The prisoner is a violent excitable woman. She was punished before trial for a violent assault on the Matron and since the trial she has been unwell from excitement but has conducted herself better.' Ann Docherty was sentenced to seven years penal servitude after being convicted in Newcastle on 17 October 1878 of stealing a silver watch from a John Minikin. Her previous convictions for fraud in Edinburgh counted against her; before becoming a prisoner in Newcastle Prison, she had served no fewer than eight terms of imprisonment, under the aliases Cuff or Wood.

Conditions at the Prison would not have helped recruitment. In 1850 a matron and an assistant matron from Scotland spoke of Newcastle Gaol as the worst they had ever seen. It was often easier to employ the wives of male staff; for example, in 1833 the matron was the turnkey's wife. However, even that was no guarantee of stability. In March 1840 Richard Goulding became assistant turnkey and his wife Hannah was appointed as the under matron. When the matron Mrs Somerville resigned in August 1840, Hannah Goulding became the next matron. Her assistant matron was Mary Loggan, wife of the assistant turnkey Edward Loggan. In November 1840, Mr and Mrs Loggan resigned. The next year, while Hannah Goulding was still matron, the assistant matron was Ann Armstrong.

By 1871 the numbers of female staff of the Gaol had increased:

matron Margaret Turner (born in Ireland) was assisted by a deputy matron, Elizabeth Longlands, and three sub-matrons, all from the local area. In 1901, the matron was Emma Parish, a widow aged 49 who was born in Suffolk. She had the assistance of three warders, five assistant warders – all single women, aged between 25-43 - and one temporary assistant warder, the only married member of the female staff. By 1911, the matron Jane Meredith was assisted by seven 'prison wardresses', again all single women aged 26-42. Meredith's career reveals what was possible for a woman in the prison service, which she joined aged 24 as assistant warder at Leicester prison. She moved to prisons in Manchester, Norwich, Derby, Liverpool and Maidstone, being promoted to chief warder at Liverpool, then matron at Newcastle in 1910. She remained at Newcastle until 1919 when she was promoted to chief warder at Holloway in London.

Interestingly, only two of the women employed as warders in 1911 are recorded as working at the Prison in 1901, suggesting a high turnover of female staff, at least at that level. Pay and conditions might have been an issue. After prisons were nationalised in 1877, all prison staff became civil servants and salaries were standardised, with female officers generally receiving around £15-20 per year less than their male equivalents, on pay scales which would change little for over 40 years. There was also an expectation (if not always a requirement) that female prison staff would be unmarried: all the Newcastle Prison female officers listed in the 1921 census were single. Single female officers usually lived in the prison or in prison quarters. Many women would have left the service to marry.

The uniform of the female warders is seen in the photograph from 1925, including a white bonnet tied under the chin, which is similar to one in the nineteenth century, shown in the image on the following page.

When Newcastle Prison closed in 1925, the seven female staff remained in the prison service; three transferred to Durham and four to the women's prison at Holloway in London.

A sketch of the Chief Warder at Pentonville Prison and, right, the Principal Matron at the Female Convict Prison in Brixton.

Prison Warders

The 1925 photograph shows the Chief Officer AH Todkill, standing behind the governor, and a photo inset of Principal Officer J Stoves. Behind them stand several other unnamed prison warders wearing uniform, with caps remarkably like the cap worn by the chief warder in the nineteenth century image (left). The uniform was similar to the police uniform, except the cap. These men were the front-line staff, with day-to-day contact with the prisoners.

The chief warder was supported by lower-ranking or more junior warders, appointed by the governor. After 1877, below the chief warder was the principal warder, then warders of various classes, and then assistant warders. Seniority was indicated by badges and embroidered insignia on their uniform.

Hours worked by warders varied from prison to prison, and between governors, but shifts were usually long. Some aspects of the job appear strange to modern readers; the report of a visit to the Gaol by the *Newcastle Journal* in 1862 mentioned officers wearing felt slippers to noiselessly patrol the corridors. The work was hard, and conditions were often poor, which impacted on recruitment. Newcastle Gaol was regularly under-staffed, although this varied across time. In 1879 the newspaper account of 'A Prisoner's Life in Newcastle Gaol' reported that Governor Robins and Deputy Governor Little were supported in the male wing by a chief warder and 'a dozen ordinary warders of whom about seven only are available for the ordinary supervision of prisoners.' The same prisoner made clear his views on the working conditions of those employed in the Prison:

'The position of a warder I should judge is not much of an improvement on that of the prisoners under him: he has long hours, Sunday work, and is by no means overpaid, considering the great responsibility which rests upon him, the temptations to infidelity with which he is beset, and the constant risk of personal injury he undergoes.'

Pay was lower for warders in local prisons than for warders in convict prisons. Some prisons provided housing, but Newcastle was slow to do this; in 1890 Newcastle Prison provided accommodation only for the chief warder. Where warders lived with their families outside the prison walls, the gaol helped with finding accommodation nearby. If the warder left or was dismissed, his housing was lost too.

Being a prison warder was not an easy job. Throughout the time the Prison was open, newspapers carried reports of inmates found hanging in their cells after committing suicide (most often by attaching clothing or ropes from their hammock bed to a ventilation grating above the cell door): in most cases, it was a warder who discovered the body, when doing their rounds of the cells. There were also regular instances of violence. Newspapers report several attacks by inmates on warders, some serious. In 1849 a prison officer was hit on the head with a hammer being used for breaking stones by a prisoner called Ross during an outbreak of violence in the stone-breaking yard. In 1886, John Cunningham, a 33-year-old stonemason, serving a 15-month sentence for stealing a watch, was charged with attempting to murder warder Thomas Wallace. About 6.50 am on 19 May, Wallace opened a door and heard something whizzing past his ear, 'on turning round he saw the prisoner with a stone in his hand with which he struck him a violent blow' on the top of his head. Wallace was hit again, and they struggled, but Wallace was able to hold Cunningham off until assistance arrived. Wallace suffered a cut on the top of his head and several wounds to his face and neck. Another warder reported that Cunningham had struck Wallace three or four times with the stone. Cunningham pleaded guilty to unlawful wounding and was sentenced to a further 15 months.

Cunningham remained a danger to prison staff. In 1887, he attacked the chief warder, John Graham, violently knocking him to the ground, causing severe injuries to his head and arm. Charged with wounding with intent to cause grievous bodily harm, Cunningham was found not guilty, because the prison surgeon could not confirm whether Graham's injuries were caused by Cunningham or by Graham falling to the ground after the attack.

Warders had various occupations before joining the prison service. Turnover was higher than for more senior roles. Yet despite the dangers of the job, some men served as warders at Newcastle for their entire career. The salary, allowances and prospects for promotion or advancement can be seen in the career of Thomas Barrett. Barrett joined Newcastle Prison as an assistant warder in 1887, aged 24. His salary was £60-68 per annum and from 1891 he also received an allowance of £9 per annum towards his lodgings and £5.4 shillings per annum for uniform. Thomas was promoted to warder at Newcastle Prison in 1895, after nearly eight years as assistant warder; his salary rose to £70-78 per annum. In 1897 he became a Clerk and Schoolmaster (C&S) warder, with an additional annual allowance; in 1912 he was promoted to C&S Grade I, with a salary of £100-120 per annum. He retired in 1921, aged 60. Harry Bartle, governor of Newcastle Prison 1901-10 started his career as a warder, and John Hallsey, acting governor at Newcastle Prison in 1919-20 was previously chief warder at the Prison.

Taskmaster

Over time, ordinary prison warders began to carry out roles that were previously specific jobs within the gaol. One example is the taskmaster, whose role is obvious from the name. In terms of seniority, he was below the governor, chaplain and surgeon, but his role was arguably more important in the day-to-day running of the gaol and oversight of the prisoners and their work than anyone bar the governor. In September 1836 John Smith, aged 30 and unmarried, was elected as under taskmaster of the House of Correction. By 1841 John Smith was the principal taskmaster, and working alongside a new under taskmaster James Hadfield, aged 45 and previously a soldier in the Royal Artillery. The following year, Hadfield was promoted from under taskmaster to principal turnkey, a position he held for some years. Hadfield's replacement as under taskmaster in 1842 was Robert Goulding, formerly the assistant turnkey.

Turnkeys

Originally turnkeys were the prison officers charged with keeping prisoners securely in their cells. They unlocked cell doors each morning and ensured prisoners were locked in at night. Another function of the turnkey was to accompany convicts from the gaol to ships on the Tyne where they would board to sail to the hulks in the south of England to await transportation to Australia. When prisoners escaped, the turnkey was often held responsible. When an escape occurred in 1852, despite the principal turnkey having bolted cell doors, he was lucky to keep his job. However, in 1860, after another prison escape, the turnkey was suspended.

The turnkey had an assistant, a junior role. In December 1836 an advertisement was placed by the Town Council in the *Newcastle Journal* for 'a young man to act as assistant turnkey and messenger.' Surviving records show who filled that role in January 1837 and his salary. However, the job was re-advertised in September 1837, and again in July 1840, when an assistant turnkey was 'wanted immediately.'

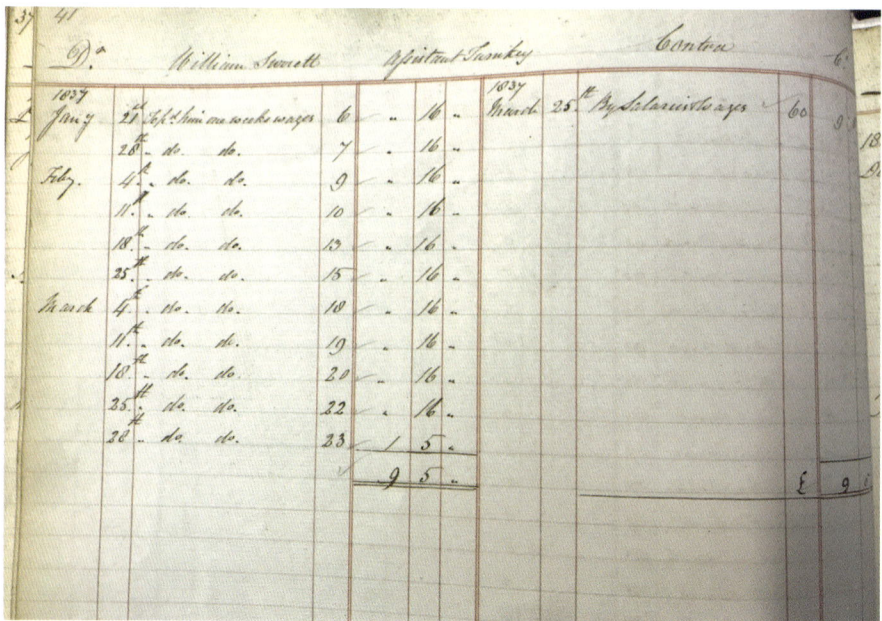

Salary of Assistant Turnkey in 1837.

Porter

Another role which later came under the general duties of the warders was that of porter. In 1836 Porter Christopher Rowell was paid 16s per week. He was still in post in 1842. His wife Ann was the searcher of female visitors. When Christopher died in 1843 Ann also lost her job and her accommodation: the Gaol immediately advertised for a 'steady active Married Couple, without Family, for the Situations of Porter and Female Searcher.'

The 'searcher' performed an important role. Anyone visiting inmates was searched before the meeting could take place. The 'Additional Rules of the Gaol' (1830) provided that keepers would search male visitors but only the matron could search female visitors, although she could appoint another woman as female searcher. The story of Ann Rowell suggests that this role was delegated by the matron to the wife of the porter.

Clerks

Clerks were employed at the Prison. One is shown in the photograph from 1925, smart in civilian clothes, holding his hat. The term 'clerk' generally referred to someone who worked in an office, providing administrative support for the running of the gaol. This could include making written entries or records, keeping accounts, dealing with the mechanical work of correspondence and other similar administrative tasks.

Not all clerks at the Prison were respectable. On 20 October 1880 Robert Joseph Twizell, a clerk, pleaded guilty to embezzling £5 13s 6d on 24 March 1880 and a further £10 on 24 May 1880, 'the money of Her Majesty.' Mr Walton, Twizell's lawyer, asked the Court to give Twizell a lenient sentence because 'he had always had a good character.' To no avail: Twizell was sentenced to six months imprisonment with hard labour, despite his good references. Mr Walton asked if Twizell could go to a different prison rather than to Newcastle, but the judge declined, saying he had no power to order that, leaving Twizell to face the prospect of ending up an inmate in the prison where he previously worked.

Conclusion

The photograph at the head of chapter gives a brief snapshot of the staff at the Prison. Sadly, we have not found any other similar photographs. Many men and women were responsible for the day to day running of the prison, some who stayed and left their mark on the inmates and others who spent a fleeting time. Unless they were mentioned on the ten yearly census, or their names were associated with events in the prison in the newspapers, their role is forgotten. Having looked at the staff, the next chapter focuses on the women inmates.

CHAPTER 4

THE WOMEN'S GAOL

In 1855 John Irwin, the chaplain of the Gaol, became concerned that the continued poor state of the place made it impossible to reform the prisoners. Irwin used the situation in the women's prison particularly to highlight the failings of the system, as he saw them,

'What right have we, because a young girl commits a brawl in the streets, and is too poor to pay the fine, or sells oranges on the footpath, or steals her mistress's lace collar - her first offence - to shut her up, bolted and barred and locked in night and day with the vilest, the most hardened, the most abandoned of her sex - women from whose contact she would have shrunk with a shudder had she met them in the street.'

His view of the women prisoners in Newcastle was shared by at least one member of the Town Council, who called them a 'deplorable set of wretches'.

Who were the women held in Newcastle Gaol, and what was life like for them?

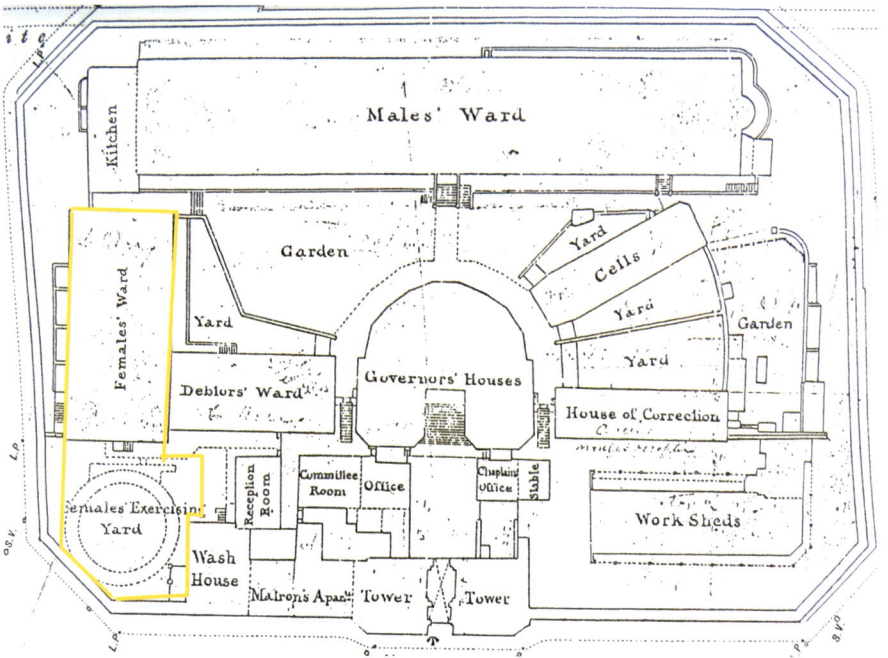

A plan of the Gaol showing the Women's Ward.

THE WOMEN'S WING

In 1862, the *Newcastle Journal* published a fascinating account of a tour of the new women's wing, which was built on the same plan as the accommodation for the male prisoners, only, according to the journalists, 'being smaller and still better lighted – indeed, we imagine that in summer the glare of light through its glass roof and end will be almost painful'. The amount of glass used can be seen in this reconstruction of the women's wing.

The Women Prisoners

Women prisoners lived in separate accommodation and exercised away from the men, as shown on the plan. The location of the women's wing changed each time the Gaol was remodelled. In 1862, the women's wing was enlarged to provide single occupancy cells for 70 female prisoners. At times even this was not enough. The number of women in the Gaol varied from around 20-30 prisoners in the 1840s, peaking around the 1880s when there were over 80 women in the Gaol at a time. The numbers fell to 50-60 at the turn of the century, and dropped again to around 30-50 in the 1910s-20s. The women's wing was moved in 1862, to the north west side of the Gaol, nearer to Carliol Street where the building was visible to outsiders as it ran parallel with the west wall. It was close to the site where executions were carried out. In 1863 Governor Thomas Robins decided to move the site for the next execution because he feared the 'effect which the tragedy might have upon the minds of the female prisoners.'

Newcastle Gaol was known for its unusually high number of female offenders. Women made up almost one-third of committals in 1865/66; by contrast, elsewhere, women generally made up around a quarter of those committed to county and borough prisons c.1850-1900. Most of the women prisoners were from the poor or working classes. Governor Robins blamed the high numbers of women offenders in his gaol on the lack of demand for female labour in the region, unlike the North West, he said, where women could work in the textile industries.

Most of the women in Newcastle Gaol had committed petty crimes, including theft and offences related to prostitution, drunkenness and other types of disorderly behaviour, often linked to poverty. Many women inmates were locked-up when they could not afford to pay a fine imposed by the magistrates. Most were serving short sentences, of days, weeks or months; few were sentenced to a year or more (this was typical of a local prison, and during the second half of the nineteenth century, around 98% of all women sentenced to imprisonment went to local prisons). Other women may have been held on remand before trial, or before being taken to another gaol, perhaps a convict prison for a long sentence, or while waiting to be transported or even while awaiting execution. The turnover of inmates was high. The women passing through Newcastle Gaol had little time for 'reform' or education.

Most women held in the Gaol were from the local area. For example, in April 1881, 85 women were incarcerated, meaning even the enlarged wing was overcrowded. Of these, nine had been born in Ireland, and eight in Scotland; there was also one born in Norway and one in Germany; the rest were from Newcastle or the surrounding areas. Not all the women gave their occupation, but five were described as domestic servants – an option usually available only if you had experience or references - and six were charwomen, who cleaned homes on a casual basis. Four were 'factory women'. 10 were hawkers who sold goods in the street, which was often seen as a last alternative to the workhouse. This pattern was largely repeated 10 years later. In April 1891, there were 69 women prisoners, meaning the women's wing was almost at full capacity. Seven were from Ireland and seven from Scotland, two from Norway and one from the Shetland Islands (which could be due to links with the fishing industry). 38 listed their occupation: seven were charwomen, five domestic servants, nine factory workers and nine hawkers. In April 1901, of 59 women prisoners, not all gave occupations, but the numbers and options remain similar and limited - five charwomen, 11 domestic servants, and eight hawkers - alongside the more unusual street singer and rag gatherer. That the occupations of the women remained similar shows how limited the employment opportunities were for poor and working-class women in the North East. By the 1910s and 1920s, most of the women prisoners were from Newcastle or the local area. The number born in Ireland fell dramatically. And the jobs the women had been doing before they went to prison had changed too. Although domestic servants, charwomen and hawkers still predominated, some women had worked on farms, in factories, or as barmaids, 'tailoresses' and milliners. Whether they would be able to return to any of these occupations after they were released is unknown.

Many of the women prisoners were married, and many had children. Some women sent to the Gaol took their young children with them. The image shows women with their children exercising at a correctional prison in London - the scene would have been very similar at Newcastle Gaol. Looking after babies and young children in cells must have been difficult, although the guarantee of food and daily access to the surgeon and chaplain may have offered more structure and support in their lives than some had outside the Prison.

Mothers and their children exercising in Tothill Fields Prison.

One of these women was Mary Jane Dawson. In March 1881, she was charged, alongside Hugh Hassan, with stealing a purse containing 26 shillings from a young man from Gateshead, 'while in the Back Row on Sunday night'. Hassan was a bricklayer's labourer born in Ireland, aged 29. Mary Jane was aged 28 and unmarried, a white lead factory worker (possibly at the Elswick Lead Works). Found guilty, Hassan was sent to prison for two months, and Mary Jane was sentenced to three months. Newspaper reports of her trial and conviction did not mention that she was pregnant, but she must have been because when she went to prison, she took her baby son Hugh with her. She was one of six women prisoners who had their children with them at that time, all aged under one; three were under three months old. From the boy's name, we can assume Hassan was the boy's father, and Mary Jane Dawson and Hugh Hassan were married in Newcastle late in 1885.

Women of all ages were sent to Newcastle Gaol. At one point in 1851, of the 29 women prisoners, six were aged 16 or under. Three had been convicted together of the same crime. Anne Kelly (16), Sarah Cain (15) and Mary Henry (15) pleaded guilty at the Newcastle Quarter Sessions on 9 April 1851 to stealing 18 towels. The *Newcastle Courant* reported that despite their young age, all had previously appeared before the magistrates and had been convicted several times.

Their stories bear out the concerns of Samuel Thompson, governor of the Gaol at the time, who said: 'I have rarely known a poor boy or girl, committed to this prison whether for a long or a short period who has not become a frequent inmate of its walls.' Sarah Cain had been convicted by the magistrates four times since March 1850. In January 1851, she had been sentenced to 14-days imprisonment for being found in the yard of a property 'for an unlawful purpose'. In April that same year, aged 15, she was sentenced to six months imprisonment. Sarah Cain was not reformed by her two terms in Newcastle Gaol in 1851: in 1854 she was sentenced to another week in prison for trying to steal a pot of bear's grease from a stall at the fair, and the police described her as a known shoplifter.

MARGARET ANN O'BRIEN

'Margaret Ann O'Brien (14), 1 Queen's Terrace, North Shields, was remanded for eight days for attempting to obtain from Messrs Irvin & Son's office the sum of £1, with intent to cheat and defraud them, on the 5th August.' (*Shields Daily News* 6 August 1904).

In court, Margaret presented a problem for the magistrates, who thought she did not seem to understand what theft was, even though she was arrested after her third (unsuccessful) attempt to get money from the same firm of fishing boat owners. Each time she said the money was for a Mrs Davies, the wife of an engineer on one of Irvin & Son's boats. In the end, the magistrates decided, 'to inflict a punishment upon her which it was hoped would have the effect of reclaiming her from the career in which she had started'. Aged only 14, she was sent to Newcastle Prison.

Mary Henry was the second girl sent to Newcastle Gaol for the theft. She also had previous minor convictions, six since August 1849. In April 1851, Henry, aged 15, was sentenced to six months imprisonment. Like Cain, Henry was not put off further offending by her time in prison. When she was convicted of breaking into a house and stealing property in 1855 her previous conviction counted against her, and she was sentenced to four years in prison. Such a long sentence would not have been served in Newcastle; she would have been transferred to a convict prison.

The third girl who pleaded guilty to stealing towels was Ann Kelly. Although she was only 16, she also had previous convictions – but unlike the other girls, one of Kelly's convictions had been for a more serious offence. In October 1850, Kelly had pleaded guilty and was convicted of larceny and sentenced to three months imprisonment. This counted against her at her trial in 1851; the magistrates decided that Kelly had had a chance but 'appeared impossible to reform', so she was dealt with severely: she was sentenced to be transported for seven years. She arrived in Van Diemen's Land in January 1852. Most female convicts transported to Van Diemen's land would have spent at least some time in the Cascades Female Factory in Hobart. At first, Ann Kelly did not find life easy: she was sentenced to one-month hard labour for refusing to work, with three days of bread and water and working 'at the wash tub.' But she served her sentence and gained her freedom. She settled into life in Australia, marrying James Oliver, a transported convict; they had five children, and Ann died there in 1882.

Painting of Cascades Female Factory in Hobart, Tasmania, where many female convicts were sent.

Although many young girls sent to Newcastle Gaol became repeat offenders and were imprisoned several times, sometimes they had a chance to reform outside the gaol. After the Youthful Offenders Act was passed in 1854, children aged under 18 would be sent to prison for a maximum of 14 days and would then be transferred to a Reformatory School for 2-5 years. In February 1891, Jemima Brown was aged 13 when she was convicted of stealing two pairs of boots in Tynemouth in December 1890 and January 1891. One pair of boots had in fact been stolen by her younger brother, aged nine, but he was discharged by the magistrates. Sadly, Jemima and her brother were then charged with stealing several purses from a shop window in North Shields in March 1891. A police superintendent described Jemima as 'a trained thief'. At her trial in April, Jemima – described as having no education – pleaded guilty to two charges of theft and was sentenced to 10 days imprisonment in Newcastle Gaol's women's wing. On her release, she was sent to a reformatory for five years, 'where she would be taught and instructed and the Bench hoped she would try to lead an honest life.' The approach seemed to work, as there is no record that she reoffended.

This approach was part of moves towards education and reform or rehabilitation of prisoners by the later-nineteenth century. By the 1900s an active Visiting Committee to the Gaol was working to improve conditions for the women, including arranging regular lectures. But the failure of attempts at reform is clear from the stories of women who continually reoffended and returned to Newcastle Gaol many times. In an extreme case, one woman appeared before Newcastle magistrates 250 times between c.1880-1926. She was charged - under several aliases - with many different offences, including being drunk and disorderly, fighting, wilful damage, assault on police, obstruction, assault, obscene language, importuning, theft (sometimes of money, sometimes of goods or items of clothing). Her sentences were usually of between one and three-months imprisonment, with hard labour. Many of the convictions involved alcohol: on 24 October 1894, she was released after a one month sentence for being drunk and disorderly; the next day, she was again convicted of being drunk and disorderly and returned to prison for another one month sentence.

Alcohol was the source of reoffending for many of the women prisoners. Adeline Richardson Simpson (age 39) was released on Thursday 14 July 1921 after serving nine months for obtaining whisky by false pretences – she knocked at doors as early as 3.45am and asked for whisky or brandy for people who were supposed to be ill. Only one week later, on Thursday 21 July, she appeared in court again, on another charge of obtaining whisky by false pretences, using the same modus operandi, and was sentenced to another six months in prison.

Life in the Women's Wing

Conditions for the women prisoners obviously changed across the almost 100 years the Gaol was open. Each governor could make changes in the prison regime, and changes in the law had an impact, for example in 1865, when the prison regime became harsher, in 1877 when prisons were nationalised, and in 1898 when reform of prisoners became the main goal of imprisonment. For most of the time the single cell system operated for women as well as men. The women were confined to their cells for much of the day, alone. Meals were eaten in their cells. For many, used

Typical cell in a Victorian prison, with hammock bed.

to sharing cramped and crowded accommodation outside the gaol, this solitude and silence would have been a frightening experience. Yet at times the Gaol was so overcrowded women would have had to share a small cell designed for sole occupation. Women prisoners were allowed out of their cells to get some limited exercise, usually walking around in a separate exercising yard. This was not a time for free association, they were closely supervised by the prison staff, as is seen in the story of Margaret Benson, told in this chapter.

Cells were small but had enough space for the women to work. Instead of stone-breaking like the male prisoners, women were given other tasks, such as housekeeping activities and needlework. Some would be consigned to hard labour, including picking oakum and laundry work. The image shows women working in a laundry at a convict prison in London - the scene would likely have been similar at Newcastle. Laundry duty was notoriously hard, hot and dangerous. The first woman inspector of prisons Dr Mary Gordon wrote in 1922 that she was 'surprised to find that hard labour meant an exceedingly moderate day's work in scrubbing, or at the wash tub.'

Female convicts on laundry duty.

Surprisingly, it was male prisoners who worked in the kitchens, cooking food for all inmates. Women prisoners would be given their food without any communication taking place between them and the men.

The diet for women prisoners was usually similar to what the men ate, but 'on a slightly reduced scale'. Male prisoners were fed roughly one pint of gruel and 6oz bread for breakfast; dinner would be something like ½lb potatoes or ½ pint soup or 1 pint gruel, and 6oz bread. If the women had this on a 'slightly reduced scale', it would be a very meagre diet indeed, although it is a sobering thought that some of the women might have been used to eating something similar in their lives outside.

Prison diet varied over the nineteenth and early twentieth centuries. Food – or the lack of it - could also be used by the authorities as punishment, as was seen in the case of the suffragettes held in Newcastle Gaol.

The Suffragettes

It is impossible to discuss the women's wing of Newcastle Gaol without addressing the treatment of members of the women's suffrage movement who were held there after the so-called 'Battle of Newcastle' in October 1909. When the Chancellor, David Lloyd George, visited Newcastle, members of the Women's Social and Political Union ('suffragettes') protested at the failure of his government to give women the right to vote. They threw stones at the official cars and at the windows of several premises, including the Liberal Club, General Post Office, and Palace Theatre. 12 women were arrested and were sentenced to up to one month in Newcastle Prison. Some went on hunger strike and faced the ordeal of force-feeding.

Dorothy Pethick was sentenced to 14 days hard labour, for throwing stones at Newcastle General Post Office. She refused food for two days and on her third day, in the prison hospital, three doctors, the prison matron and a wardress forced her into a chair. She was tied down and the doctor fed her egg and milk via a tube inserted in her nose, while a wardress covered her mouth. Despite vomiting, she was force-fed twice each day until her nose became inflamed. She served her full 14-day sentence in Newcastle and was released on 23 October 1909. After her release she wrote in Votes for Women about the poor hygiene practices she had witnessed as part of the force-feeding ordeal.

The General Post Office building in Newcastle, which was attacked by suffragettes in 1909.

Possibly the best-known of the suffragettes force-fed in Newcastle Prison was Kitty Marion, an actress and music hall singer. Her first sentence of imprisonment was in Newcastle Prison in October 1909, when she was sentenced alongside Dorothy Pethick for throwing a stone at the General Post Office window. Once in the Prison, she barricaded herself into her cell and went on hunger strike. Her description of being force-fed through a nasal tube is harrowing. She recalled choking and vomiting. Later she set a fire in her cell, so a wardress was set outside to keep watch. She served a month's hard labour and was released on 10 November 1909.

It is interesting that many of the suffragettes imprisoned in Newcastle praised the staff. Lady Constance Lytton recalled the governor telling them how keen he was for women to have the vote, and that he seemed very glad when they were to be released. She described the matron as 'considerate and kind in all her ways.' Perhaps most interesting is that she was, 'pleased to notice that the prisoners who worked outside the cells moved happily, ran about with a springing step and seemed like ordinary servants about their work. How different this was from Holloway!'

Kitty Marion's account of her time in Newcastle Prison revealed that several members of the staff - including the governor, the matron, the doctor, the chaplain and the schoolmistress - had at some point tried to visit her in her cell. Despite slapping a doctor during her force-feeding ordeal, Marion said she was treated with sympathy when she took small amounts of food. The prison medical officer Dr William Hardcastle told her he considered tube feeding 'demoralising and degrading' but that he could not let her starve or he would be guilty of manslaughter. Marion said she was treated with care and kindness by the staff.

Although some of the staff tried to create a positive environment for some women inmates, Newcastle Gaol faced many problems with discipline.

Discipline

Different punishments for indiscipline were used for women prisoners and male prisoners. Women were not whipped or flogged, as men were, nor were women put on the treadmill after 1820-30s, which meant that other disciplinary measures were used. This can be seen in the story of one prisoner, Margaret Benson.

On 3 January 1855, Benson was convicted of larceny and was sentenced to nine months in Newcastle. She had stolen a purse containing about £20 from John Winship, an 'elderly man' (aged about 64), an unmarried farmer from Wark in Northumberland. He told the court he was accosted by a young girl (Benson) in Clayton Street about 2.30pm, who asked him to treat her to a

LADY CONSTANCE LYTTON

Lady Constance Lytton was a suffragette who was not force-fed in Newcastle Gaol. Convicted of 'disorderly behaviour with intent to disturb the peace' after throwing a stone at an official car, she was sentenced to one month's imprisonment in Newcastle Gaol in 1909. Lytton went on hunger strike but was released after a few days - a doctor confirmed that her heart was too weak for her to be force-fed. Lady Constance complained that she had received better treatment than other suffragettes held in Newcastle, and suspected it was because of her name and title. Her suspicions were confirmed in 1910, when she disguised herself as 'Jane Warton', a woman of lower social standing: she was convicted and force-fed in a prison in Liverpool.

glass. He said he was going to have some refreshment in a cook shop; she followed him, and they had two plates of goose. They were there for about half an hour. Winship admitted he had had some alcohol, but said he was not incapable. When he left the room, Benson followed him, and he felt her touch his left side; when she ran away, he found his purse had gone. Benson was caught, but without the purse. At her trial, a previous conviction was raised; in 1854, she had been charged with picking a man's pocket of half a sovereign and some silver. The man had been walking down St John's Lane when Benson allegedly threw her arms around him and tried to take money from his pocket. When he realised money had been taken, he found a police officer. When caught, even though nothing was found, Benson was committed for three months as a 'reputed thief.' At her trial in 1855, Benson was found guilty and sentenced to nine months with hard labour, even though again nothing was found on her.

Showering

When Newcastle Gaol was visited by the Prison Inspector on 20 August 1855, he found Margaret Benson in a 'dark cell.' She complained that she was there as punishment for an offence which she had not committed. She said that she had been one of several women in a room overlooking the female exercise yard; they had been told not to look out of the window, but when two women started fighting in the yard - making what the Inspector termed 'the usual screaming uproar' - the matron said Benson had looked out of the window. Benson said something insulting, which the matron reported to the governor, who ordered the prisoner a shower bath. The Prison Inspector's Report described the 'shower-bath' as a 'common punishment in this prison.'

Cold-shower treatments were originally a medical treatment for insanity, the idea being that a shock of cold water on the head could calm an inflamed brain. It also had the advantage for prison authorities of inflicting physical punishment on the female criminal body without, for example, leaving the marks of a whip. We do not know exactly what form the shower bath punishment took in Newcastle Gaol, but it was evidently not without risk to the prisoner. The Prison Inspector noted that at Newcastle Gaol, 'The shower bath is never administered without the sanction of the surgeon.'

Interestingly, Governor Samuel Thompson told the Prison Inspector that the shower bath was 'a very efficacious punishment', which he could 'scarcely do without'. The Inspector disapproved - his report said that 'suitable provision ought to be made for the accommodation of the prisoners, instead of obliging the governor to resort to punishments which are not authorized by the prison rules.' Clearly, the governor of Newcastle Gaol recognised that he operated outside the prison rules using the shower bath so regularly but felt it was necessary to keep control of the prisoners.

Punishment Cells

When Margaret Benson refused to undergo the shower bath, she was put in a 'dark cell', where the Prison Inspector found her. She told him that it was a punishment often faced by the women prisoners. But it is significant that Margaret Benson preferred the dark cell to the shower bath.

Muzzle

Benson also told the Prison Inspector about another common punishment at Newcastle in 1855: a 'muzzle'. His report said that two women prisoners were 'violently shouting, and calling out from their dormitories, and disturbing the whole prison'. As punishment for this 'gross misconduct', they were put in a head piece or muzzle, which he said, 'effectually prevents them from shouting, but allows them to respire freely.' This punishment suggests the scolds-bridle. An iron framework resembling a muzzle or cage, it was closed over the head, with a 'curb-plate' on the tongue. The women would be unable to speak, eat or drink; it would be uncomfortable and painful. In Newcastle Gaol, it was used to stop women prisoners shouting, and to punish disobedience. (They were also used on women in workhouses in the nineteenth century, for similar reasons). But the muzzle was never used on noisy male prisoners, and after its use on a woman prisoner in Shrewsbury Gaol in 1860 it was held to be illegal.

A muzzle or cage known as the scolds-bridle.

The governor of Newcastle in 1855 clearly used some unusual (and possibly illegal) methods to keep control – this might have been due to weak leadership, or the overcrowded conditions, which remained a constant problem, despite the alterations to the building and the new women's wing. After 1865, prison punishments were largely limited to reduced diet and confinement to cells.

A Condemned Woman in Newcastle Gaol

The execution of a woman prisoner was a very rare event at Newcastle, but in 1884, a woman called Sarah Jane Holmes, aged 34, was held in the Gaol under sentence of death, due to be hanged on the morning of Monday 12 May.

She had been charged with the wilful murder by poisoning of a boy aged eight or nine named John Holmes Burns at 38 Church Way, North Shields. John was the son of a solicitor's clerk who Sarah had been living with, although they were not married. Even though she was not the boy's mother, they were obviously close - he even called her 'Ma'. Newspapers reported that she had poisoned John and had attempted to poison herself. Witnesses confirmed that she had bought vermin-killer containing strychnine. The boy had drunk the glass of liquid she gave him, saying it tasted bitter. When both were found doctors could revive Sarah but not the boy.

She was tried on 25 April 1881. After deliberating in private for 15 minutes, the jury found her guilty. The penalty for murder was the death sentence. Interestingly, even though the victim was a child, there was some sympathy for Sarah. The jury strongly recommended mercy, and many people petitioned for the sentence to be commuted to life imprisonment.

Held in Newcastle before the execution, Sarah was watched constantly by two female warders, and visited daily by the prison chaplain. Her family visited when they could – even though on 7

May, her husband Thomas Holmes and her married daughter had to appear before North Shields Police Court for brawling in the streets after some words had been exchanged about Sarah. The *Shields Daily Gazette* reported that, 'Mrs Holmes never lost all hope of her life being saved.' On the morning of Thursday 8 May, a 'welcome document' was received at Newcastle Gaol from the Home Office, confirming that she would not be executed, but would be sent to prison for life instead. Jane Jamieson remained the only woman prisoner held in Newcastle to be executed.

Conclusion

Hundreds of women and girls were imprisoned behind the walls of Newcastle Gaol. As some of the women had children with them, the atmosphere in the women's wing must have been different to the men's wing. But, with hard physical labour, restricted diet, overcrowded cells and punishments used to enforce prison discipline, life for the women was no less harsh than for the men. Perhaps for that reason, some inmates were tempted to take steps to gain their freedom before they were due to be released.

CHAPTER 5

ESCAPES

Newcastle Prison was built to resemble a fortress. The few remaining images of the prison show what a dark brooding presence it was, situated close to the bustling streets of the town. There were walls within walls and a vast gate controlled by a turnkey. When first built, the prison was described as containing no wood and 'formed of nothing but stone and iron.' A journalist, who surveyed the partially-built structure in 1825, suggested that 'the person who could make his escape from it would deserve his liberty.'

Despite Dobson's attention to detail, including consulting several renowned burglars, during its nearly 100-year history, the seemingly impenetrable gaol witnessed several daring - and some not so daring - escape attempts. This chapter explores some of the ingenious and more successful escape attempts from Newcastle Prison, concluding with the story of an escape that never was. The examples discussed are not the only escapes from Newcastle Prison, but they illustrate the ingenuity and determination of inmates for whom no wall was too high and no cell too secure to deter their quest for freedom.

A Permeable Structure

One of the few preserved records from Newcastle, an account book, reveals that in addition to prisoners being transferred to and from court and staff entering and leaving through the front gate each day, the prison regularly admitted workmen, lawyers, clergy, doctors, midwives and others. At night, it was the responsibility of the staff to ensure everything was secure and that inmates were locked in their cells. With no electronic surveillance, the success of the system relied entirely on the diligence of those who designed and managed it. Although the prison operated systems that required prisoners to follow a strict daily schedule: moving from cell to chapel, to work, back to their cells, and then to exercise, the Prison was regularly short-staffed, making the task of monitoring inmates across its various wings and yards a complex challenge.

The State of the Gaol - An Incentive to Break-out

As we learned in earlier chapters, the Gaol was loud, insanitary, and dangerous. The prisoners, men, women, and children, were confined to their cells for up to 16 hours each day, only emerging for chapel or 'work,' which typically involved breaking stones or picking oakum. Given these conditions, it is perhaps unsurprising that night warders occasionally failed to make their rounds as required. The cacophony of 'shouts, songs, and blasphemies' often masked the sounds of determined individuals attempting, and at times succeeding, to break out. The newspapers reported escapes, both successful and unsuccessful in lurid detail. For example, in April 1834, the *Tyne Mercury* noted that five convicts had attempted to escape on several occasions. On Sunday 13 April, using a mallet fashioned from melted-down lead and rudimentary chisels made from lengths of iron, they almost succeeded. However, their plan ultimately failed and they were apprehended, placed in iron chains, and kept under close observation for the remainder of their sentences.

1843: Samuel Chapman's Escape

One of the early successful escapees was Samuel (or William) Chapman (or Mea), a brewer, aged 38, married with six children, accused of five embezzlement charges and described as 'a notorious character'. He was tall (5 feet 9 inches/1.75 metres): most of the male prisoners in the records from the early nineteenth century are recorded as under 5 feet 5 inches [1.66 metres]. A reward was offered for his recapture (identifying him as much younger than his actual age).

The prison uniform, described in the appeal for information, consisted of a grey jacket, waistcoat, trousers, and a Scotch cap: an outfit that sounded both smart and practical. However, the cap was likely the first item Chapman discarded. Unlike the jaunty bonnet commonly associated with a piper, the Scotch cap was a leather hood with eye holes, designed to prevent prisoners from communicating with each other in the Separate System.

Chapman, and five other prisoners, had been let out of their cells to wash. They decided to take the opportunity to escape by climbing the wall of the yard and dropping down into the prison garden. Their actions were soon observed and the alarm was raised. The governor and the turnkeys secured what they assumed to be all the fleeing men and returned them to their cells. Unbeknown to the staff, however, Chapman remained hidden and his absence was missed when the prisoners were counted. When the coast was clear, he used a ladder and ropes, which had been left in the yard by workmen, to get over the outer wall. In the inquiry by magistrates that followed, it was found that Chapman's escape was facilitated by the negligence of the prison staff. The competence of the governor was called into question and there were calls, led by journalists in the local newspapers, for him to be suspended. The police were criticised for not managing to capture Chapman, although the *Newcastle Journal* placed the blame squarely on the governor, whom it described as 'culpable in the extreme.' Following a tip-off, an officer from the local police force, PC Crake, was sent to Wales to find Chapman, but he returned empty handed. It was accepted that Chapman had evaded the rather half-hearted attempts to find him and escaped to America.

Prisoner in Scotch cap.

However, this was not the case. In February 1845, Governor Samuel Thompson was contacted by the gaol in Bury St Edmunds regarding a prisoner named Samuel Jackson. Upon travelling to Bury St Edmunds, Thompson discovered that 'Samuel Jackson' was in fact Samuel Chapman. Chapman confessed and revealed that, after escaping from Newcastle, he fled to Blyth on the Northumberland coast, then to Scotland, London, and finally Wales. PC Crake had been closer to recapturing Jackson than he realised.

Chapman served his sentence in Bury St Edmunds, where he again tried to escape by dismantling part of the wall of his cell. Eventually he was returned to Newcastle to be tried for the original felonies. He was found guilty and sentenced to three months hard labour followed by seven years transportation. The last record of Chapman in England is in Millbank penitentiary in 1845 before he was transported to Van Diemen's Land in December of the same year.

It seems that after the Chapman escape, and the censure of the staff by the local magistrates, the Gaol tightened its processes and there was no further reported escape until 1857.

1857: Four Desperadoes

In 1857, there was a breakout from the gaol that took advantage of lapses in the running of Newcastle Gaol that had recently been described by prison inspector Sir John Kincaird as 'a nursery for crime rather than a house for the correction of criminals.' The men involved were William Hay(e)s Beaumont, John Harris, Blakeson Hind(e) and George Winship. All four were on remand waiting to be tried at the summer assizes.

It is clear from the descriptions of the men in the newspapers, and records of their previous convictions that the four escapees were habitual criminals and 'well-known lawless characters'. Three of the men were accused of a crime that struck fear in the population in the 1850s: garrotting. Garrotting robbers usually worked in pairs or threes. *Cornhill Magazine* described the method:

'[a] ruffian flings his right arm round the victim, striking him smartly on the forehead. Instinctively he throws his head back, and in that movement loses every chance of escape. His throat is fully offered to his assailant, who instantly embraces it with his left arm, the bone just above the wrist being pressed against the 'apple' of the throat.'

While the garrotter held his victim in this grip, an accomplice stole his belongings. It was a terrifying image.

William Hayes Beaumont was a ticket of leave man on licence from having been transported. He was charged with garrotting and robbing a man in Arthur's Hill, in the west end of Newcastle. Blakeson Hind and George Winship, together with a third man, William Wise, who turned Queen's evidence and provided the police with a statement admitting the robbery and explaining the role of each man, were accused of attacking and robbing a clerk, William Oley, in the Cattle Market on 26 December 1856. Winship was a violent man who had resisted arrest and had to be bound with rope when he was apprehended. The fourth member of the group was John Harris, who was accused of attempting to kill his common-law wife in the Ouseburn area of Newcastle.

Beaumont, Harris, Hind and Winship were described as four of the most desperate men in the Gaol. They were part of an 'unexpected gaol delivery' which may have meant that the prison was not ready to deal with such violent men. They do not seem to have planned their escape in advance but to have taken advantage of an opportunity presented to them. On the day of the prison break, the men had been let out of their cells to speak to their lawyer, and the assistant warder, who had been given the task of returning the men to their cells, forgot to do so due to confusion between him and the chief warder (who had gone into town on business). The men were left in the prison yard. Despite a seemingly golden opportunity, escape was not straightforward. Although the men were not locked in their cells, they still had to get onto and over the outside wall. The images of the prison, reimagined as part of our project, graphically illustrate the height of the wall and the drop that any escapee would have faced before landing on the street.

A local reporter managed to speak to the staff at the Gaol and was able to report full details of the escape. The men fashioned ropes from torn bedding and used them to climb to the top of the wall. They then lowered themselves some 20 feet [6 metres] to the street below and melted into the night. The escape was discovered, not by a warder on his rounds but by a policeman on his 2am beat who noticed the rope on the pavement. Descriptions of the men were telegraphed to neighbouring towns with pleas for information.

Newcastle Prison. c.1925.

Once the news of the escape broke out, the Newcastle police and the new detective force swung into action. Chief Constable Sabbage, the officer in charge of the Newcastle force, was tipped off that the men had split up on gaining their freedom and a woman accomplice had fled with Beaumont and Harris. The intelligence suggested the woman had a money order and would be looking to cash it. Inspector John Elliott of the detective force set off in pursuit. Elliott soon picked up the trail and tracked the men to Carlisle, some 60 miles from Newcastle. He contacted Chief Constable Dunne of the County Constabulary and Superintendent Bent of the Carlisle police to agree a plan to recapture the fugitives. The police officers identified a post office that could be used to cash the money order and Elliott waited there for the escapees' female companion. When she arrived, he followed her to where Beaumont and Harris were hiding, preparing to flee to Wales. One of the men is reported to have said, 'this is the last day you would have had any chance of getting us, as we were going out of the country'. The escapees were in poor condition, shoeless, and worn down by their journey, with badly injured ankles caused by landing after the long drop from the prison wall. Elliot captured the men 'in the twinkling of an eye' and they were taken back to Newcastle.

Beaumont was eventually freed by the court when it was decided there was insufficient evidence to try him, but Harris was less fortunate. He was found guilty of the attempted murder of his wife and sentenced to death (death recorded), however, the sentence was commuted to transportation. And, as the records of the Australian government show, in 1860 he sailed for the Swan River colony (now Perth) in Western Australia on the convict ship Palmerston.

CHIEF CONSTABLE SABBAGE

John Hooper Sabbage was the Chief Constable of Newcastle from 1857 until 1867. He lived in Oxford Street, with his wife and two sons, in a house designed by John Dobson, from which he would have been able to see the prison. He was born in London in Mile End 1818. Sabbage began his policing career in London, then moved to Manchester before serving as Superintendent of the Carlisle Police, where he was described as 'humane and judicious', and finally being appointed to head the Newcastle police in 1857. He died, aged 49, in 1867 after contracting 'a severe case of gastric fever', reportedly as a result of spending a day on his horse, carrying out police work, in wet weather. He was buried in the south-east corner of Jesmond Cemetery.

INSPECTOR JOHN ELLIOTT

Elliott was a well-known local police detective who had been a tailor. Before joining the force, he gained a reputation for assisting in catching criminals and he eventually became the chief officer of the Gateshead police. Sometimes known as 'Clencher Elliott', such was his fame that music hall songs were written about him:

The Wizard of the North; or, The Mystic Policeman.
Robert Emery (1862)

Aw've cum fresh frae Mackies' tae sing ye a sang,
Aboot a queer chap - but aw'll not keep ye lang
...
He can flee through the air like a witch on a broom,
And bring a defaulter straight back to his doom;
...
His smell is so keen that he kens wiv his nose
When a pick-pocket's near, and he's soon on his toes;
So ye light-fingered kiddies at races beware,
For the Journeyman Tailor is sure to be there.

The Cockneyfied runners of Bow Street may pine,
To think they're eclips'd by a son of the Tyne;
...
Chorus:.
He's a limb of the deevil, as sure as you're here,
For he's learn'd him the art to restore stolen gear

The second pair, Hind and Winship, were luckier – or more cunning. Rather than join the two men travelling west to Cumberland, Hind and Winship turned south and crossed the Tyne. Their prison clothes were discovered in the grounds of a tannery in Gateshead folded, labelled and addressed to 'Mr Thompson Governor of Newcastle Gaol.' With Elliott and the detective force concentrating on Carlisle, time passed and the trail from Gateshead went cold. Then, in October 1857, Hind's luck ran out. He had made it as far as Sheffield but, unfortunately for him, he was recognised in the street by a man from Gateshead who reported his whereabouts to the police. He was swiftly apprehended. Hind told his captors that he and Winship had spent a few weeks hiding in Sunderland before travelling further south, but he had parted from his companion at some point on the journey and now had no idea of Winship's whereabouts.

Hind was tried at Newcastle in December 1857. His barrister asked the jury to ignore his escape attempt when considering whether he was guilty of the robbery. Whether they took notice of this plea or not, the jury convicted him, and he was sentenced to penal servitude for 15 years. There is no record of what happened to Winship because there is no trace of him being captured or tried. Perhaps he escaped to America - the final desperado who made it to freedom.

The warders who facilitated the escape due to their negligence kept their jobs but were severely reprimanded by the town magistrates. In January 1858, Newcastle Gaol was condemned by the Prisons Inspectorate as unfit for purpose. Later that year, perhaps taking advantage of the parlous state of the gaol, Robert Boyd joined the list of escapees.

1858: An Active-looking Fellow

Robert Boyd, aged 22, had been sentenced to 6 years hard labour in July 1858, having been found guilty of a garotte robbery. He had also been charged with assaulting a woman and stealing four shillings, although the witness did not turn up at court and so the charge was dropped. Boyd's escape had similarities with the earlier break-out: it is likely that prisoners shared tips and taught each other how to make ropes from rugs and bedding.

Boyd was a prize fighter, a smuggler and a general ruffian. He was described by the newspapers as 'an active looking fellow' and perhaps for that reason he was held in a single cell in a wing overlooking the governor's residence. This location was problematic for a prospective escapee because the governor was known to be a light sleeper. However, on the night in question, perhaps because the prison was especially noisy, Boyd put into practice an audacious and complex escape plan.

The cell he was housed in included a boxed-in pipe which drained water from the roof. The pipe was sealed at the top with a zinc collar. Boyd used a chisel, likely thrown over the wall by an accomplice on the outside, to force the panels from the wall and remove the collar. He reached through the hole and removed slates from the roof before squeezing himself through the 23 cm by 38cm [9 inches by 15 inches] hole: he must have been extremely fit and lithe as he manoeuvred his 'well-built' frame through the gap.

Boyd tied his bedding to rugs taken from empty cells on his landing to make a rope and, using it to scale any barriers he encountered, managed to reach the stone-breaking yard where he found a plank and 'bags of hair'- likely to have been oakum. Where the inner wall of the prison joined the outer wall there was a row of revolving spikes, known as a cheveux de frise, and Boyd used the bags of hair to wedge the spikes to prevent them from moving. Using the plank and the rope he descended some 40 feet [12 metres] to Carliol Square. Journalists interviewed staff at the prison to elicit details of the escape, which is how we have such a detailed account of Boyd's ingenuity. Interestingly, when speaking to the journalist, the turnkey at the outer gate said that, whilst he oversaw the main gate, he had never been inside the prison.

Jack Sheppard helping an accomplice escape using knotted sheets - cheveux de frise in foreground.

It is unclear at what time of night the daring escape took place, but the window of opportunity was between 2am, when PC Oliver made his nightly beat rounds, and 3.30am when Oliver passed the prison again and found the rope and the plank. Boyd lacked distinguishing features, and it was thought by the authorities that recapture was unlikely. The newspapers reported that in criminal circles Boyd was viewed as the 'most ingenious amongst them' and they too held out little hope of capture. However, Boyd's cunning was a little lacking. Following a tip-off, the police found him staying with his brother a mere 10 miles away, in Hebburn. The Durham police lay in wait until Boyd emerged from the house to take a walk. The policemen approached and Boyd panicked and ran. He was eventually cornered and drew a life preserver. Boyd fought hard - he was a prize fighter - and severely wounded one of the officers but he was eventually overpowered and returned to his cell.

The capture was just in time because Boyd had signed as a crew member on a ship bound for America. Instead of joining the ship, he was taken to Millbank prison in London and then, in 1859, on to Portland prison in Dorset. His behaviour was described as 'good' in Millbank and 'very good' in Portland, so perhaps he learned his lesson. He was discharged on licence to his mother's address in Gateshead on 6 February 1863. He would arrive back in the North East in time for the last public hanging at the Gaol, that of George Vass on 14 March 1863.

1859: A New Jack Sheppard

In October 1859, a daring escape from Newcastle came to the attention of the Prisons' Inspectorate. Three men - Joseph Preshions, Walter Scott Douglas, and Edward Rawlins - escaped while on remand for housebreaking. The men were held in the older part of the Gaol while new wings were under construction. Using the tried-and-tested method, they fashioned a rope from bedding and hammocks to scale the prison walls and lower themselves onto the street.

Notably, all three were trained mechanics, and they executed a clever feat of engineering to break through the seemingly well-secured cell doors. The prisoners had been locked in their cells with a chain allowing the door to be partly open whilst they waited for the deputy governor to make his rounds. To check that the prisoners were well, the governor was in the habit of asking at each door 'is all right?' and afterwards the cells were secured by a heavy iron bar which locked itself into a socket in the wall. On the evening of the escape either the deputy governor received no answer or was negligent. The following morning three cells were found to be open and empty. Preshions, Douglas and Rawlings had escaped.

Preshions, who injured his leg in the fall from the wall, was soon apprehended by Chief Constable Sabbage. Rawlings evaded capture. Douglas remained free until April when Inspector Elliott and his detective colleague Selby Fawcett were patrolling

Scotswood Road, where a 'Hopping' was being held. The detectives ran into Douglas by chance. They acted swiftly and managed to pinion his hands – which was just as well because when they searched his pockets they discovered he was carrying a bullet mould, false whiskers 'of considerable dimensions', gold jewellery... and two loaded pistols.

Douglas had a high opinion of himself and was something of a celebrity. He was a 'sprightly man' with a 'habitual scowl', tall, with fair hair and a beard. The newspapers were delighted to tell their readers, he had once been a respectable and first-rate joiner, but he had been attracted to a life of crime after reading a history of Jack Sheppard, a notorious thief and prison escaper who cultivated a reputation as a glamourous rogue. Douglas had a long criminal record and, in 1855, spent some time on a prison hulk waiting to be transported, but he does not appear to have made

JACK SHEPPARD

Jack Sheppard, sometimes known as 'honest Jack', was born in Spitalfields, London, and trained as a carpenter. However, he turned to burglary and housebreaking instead of pursuing an honest trade. Despite his criminal activities, it was not his crimes that made him famous, but his extraordinary ability to escape from prison. In 1724, Sheppard managed to escape from several prisons, including Newgate, a total of four times, earning him widespread notoriety and turning him into a folk hero. His daring escapades captivated the public and inspired books, plays, and ballads. It is rumoured that Daniel Defoe wrote Sheppard's 'autobiography,' which was distributed to the crowd at his execution at Tyburn in November 1724.

the journey to Australia. On gaining his freedom he returned to Newcastle and his thieving life.

Following his recapture after the initial prison break, Douglas was brought before the magistrates and returned to the Prison to await trial at the assizes. However, Douglas was determined to emulate the infamous Jack Sheppard. On Sunday 29 April, he staged a second daring escape. Whilst the other prisoners attended chapel, Douglas remained in the dayroom to eat breakfast. Seizing the opportunity, he forced the bolt on the door and made his way into the prison yard. The yard was surrounded by a gate, 15 feet high [4.6 metres], and then the outer prison walls. Ingeniously, he used furniture from the dayroom to construct makeshift scaffolding, allowing him to scale the wall and bridge the gap between the roof of a water closet and the outer wall. After clambering over the first wall, Douglas dropped into another yard where masons, working on the new prison wings, had left stone and tools. Using a pole and rope taken from his hammock, he scaled and crossed the perimeter wall opposite the Jubilee School, where his escape was observed by the schoolmistress. The alarm was quickly raised, and within 20 minutes, 30 police officers, both uniformed and plain-clothed, were in pursuit.

The deputy governor soon received a letter, purporting to be from Douglas stating,

'by the time this reaches you I will have left the town, which I hope will be forever. I do not wish that you or any of the officers connected with the prison should be charged with neglect of duty on account of my late escape… Adieu for ever.'

No stamp was attached and therefore the governor had to pay the postage. Whether this letter was from Douglas or whether it was from a prison officer keen to protect his position and avoid dismissal is unknown. The warder charged with guarding Douglas was discharged having been accused of leaving the door to the yard insufficiently locked. The deputy governor, Mr Woods, was asked to resign, which he duly did.

SELBY FORSTER FAWCETT

Selby Forster Fawcett joined the Newcastle police in 1850 and retired in 1878 as a Detective Inspector. He worked closely with Inspector John Elliott and gained a reputation as an outstanding detective with an unrivalled knowledge of criminal behaviour. When he died in 1899 his obituary recorded that he, and Elliott, 'were held in particular detestation by criminals and ... fulfilled his duty at considerable personal risk'. One of his most prized possessions was a gold watch and Albert chain, presented on the occasion of the capture of a gang of thieves who broke into the premises of Lister and Sons, Goldsmiths, Jewellers, Watch and Clock Makers, on Grey Street. After leaving the police force, he was much in demand as a private detective.

The Warrior Prison Hulk.

On 4 May Superintendent Sabbage received news from Staindrop, in Weardale, that a man fitting Douglas' description had been taken into custody - but this was a case of mistaken identity. The trail went cold, and it seemed that Douglas had evaded capture. However, in January 1861, Sabbage and Elliott went by train to London to identify a man who called himself 'Thomas Andrews', captured in Whitechapel by the Metropolitan Police and who was suspected of being Douglas. Sabbage and Elliott returned empty handed, not because Andrews was not Douglas (he was) but because, in London, Douglas had attacked a prison guard with a sharpened spoon and the Secretary of State, Sir George Lewis, rescinded an order to send him to Newcastle for trial for the offence of prison breaking. Douglas was sentenced to ten years penal servitude. It is not known whether he ever saw Newcastle again.

1870: Escape of a Female Convict

Thus far, this chapter has discussed male escapees but Newcastle also housed women who escaped. One example is Mary O'Neil, a petty thief. In July 1870, 27-year-old O'Neil was convicted of stealing a purse containing 12 shillings. She was found guilty and sentenced to seven years penal servitude. Mary was not contrite and on being sentenced said to the judge: 'Thank you - that's not nice. It'll do me no good. I'll come back as bad as ever'. She screamed and howled, and the court had to be cleared, but she was eventually subdued and taken to a cell in the north west end of the prison.

Newcastle was not designed to hold inmates serving long sentences. Sentences of penal servitude were served in convict prisons and therefore O'Neil was being held in Newcastle only until she could be transferred. But O'Neil did not wish to be confined in the prison for any longer than was necessary. She broke an iron bar out of the window, climbed onto the roof, fastened a piece of rope to the top of the washhouse and climbed over the boundary wall near the Gaol entrance. The wall was about 25 feet [7.62 metres] high at this point, and her rope was short, so she fell a great distance, but despite this, and the fact that she must have been injured, she managed to get away.

Mary's escape was successful at first and she remained at large for longer than many of her male counterparts. She was on the run until January 1871 when she was apprehended in Liverpool, about to embark for America. Interestingly it was a photograph, perhaps taken as a mugshot, that enabled the police to recognise and catch her. Mary was sent to Woking prison in Surrey which was a new prison tailored to the redemption of female criminals. Her conduct during her imprisonment was recorded as 'very good'.

But Mary did keep her promise to the judge in Newcastle and did come back 'as bad as ever'- as Margaret Reynolds/alias O'Neil alias Collins, when she was again sent to prison in Newcastle in August 1878 for pickpocketing. This time she was sentenced to 10 years. This sentence would not have been served in Newcastle, but where she was sent to be incarcerated is unknown. There is an entry in the register of the Newcastle Lunatic Asylum in 1885 for a Mary Reynolds - but whether it is this woman is impossible to say.

The 1870s and 1880s saw few escapes from the Prison as governors Thomas Robins and William Wookey restored security and brought the prison under greater control. In 1886, John Young managed to gain his freedom for two hours after using a rope ladder that had been left in the prison yard during repairs. He was swiftly captured and returned to his cell. In the 1890s, several unsuccessful attempts to escape were made by James Thompson, serving 12 months for burglary. His escape-practice must have paid off because he later absconded from Whitehaven police station, having forced iron window bars from their stone casing. He was re-captured in Newcastle.

And Finally - The Escape That Never Was

Although most of the escapees from the prison were recaptured, a chance for freedom was an attractive prospect if a suitable opportunity presented itself. The prisoners were usually facing, once moved on from Newcastle, a long period of penal servitude or even transportation to Australia. Injury from the long fall from the perimeter wall was a risk worth taking. Having discussed some successful and not so successful escapes, the final escape discussed in this chapter is rather different - the escapee was not a garrotter, a house breaker or a thief. And his 'escape' was unusual.

In September 1914, a German engineer and inventor Johann Jurgen Kuhr, described by *The Register* as a 'wireless and explosives expert', who worked at a chemicals firm in Sunderland, was imprisoned for possessing materials that could be used for the manufacture of explosives. He had installed a research laboratory at his home in the affluent suburb of Jesmond, and was found to own a wireless telegraph, despite being denied permission by the Postmaster-General.

On 28 December 1914, the newspapers reported that Kuhr had escaped from the Prison in the early hours of the morning using the tried and tested method of making a rope from bedclothes. A wanted notice was posted throughout the country which read:

'Wanted…, John Jurgen Kuhr, German subject; …aged 45; 5ft. 5 ½in. in height; florid complexion; blue eyes, dark brown hair; proportionate build; dark brown beard, probably now shaved off; flat footed, walks bow legged; speaks imperfect English; dressed when last seen in blue serge prison clothing.'

Kuhr had given no impression of being anything other than a quiet, obedient, prisoner, so his escape was a surprise and a mystery. Police scoured the district and searched ships leaving the Tyne. All to no avail: Kuhr had vanished.

However, on 29 December, it was revealed that Kuhr had, in fact, never left the prison but had hidden in a storeroom until pangs of hunger, and pain from rheumatism, forced him to surrender. He was found to have a skeleton key in his pocket which he had used to open the prison doors. There was fear that Kuhr was a spy working for German intelligence. Whether he was or not, rather than being deported he was transferred to Reading Gaol where he was held as a prisoner of war, deemed to be 'a security risk'. His imprisonment was 'recommended by the Home Office' on the basis that MI5 had identified him as a spy. This may not have been based on concrete evidence but simply to ensure, as a man of fighting age, he was not returned to Germany. His knowledge of explosives, chemistry, telegraphy and marine engineering must have worried the authorities. Eventually Kuhr was imprisoned on the Isle of Man in Knockaloe, an internment camp that eventually held 24,000 prisoners who were mostly German and Austro-Hungarian men of fighting age. In January 1918 Kuhr was moved to a camp in Holland in preparation for release and in 1919 he is recorded as living with his family in Hamburg, where he died in 1932.

Suspected German spy Johann Jurgen Kuhr.

Conclusion

The *Newcastle Chronicle,* in 1896, suggested that for a prisoner to escape from the Prison they must be 'a crafty and adventurous individual.' Although the doors were thick and the bolts and chains strong, some inmates were able to make a bid for freedom. Most of the escapees were recaptured - but not all. In the early days when capture and recognition depended upon local knowledge, escape could be via ship or, with luck, by road. As photography became more common, and mug shots were taken, publications such as the *Police Gazette* could share images of prisoners throughout the police forces of the country. Sometimes it was detective work that recaptured the prisoners, but sometimes it was simply a case of luck running out for the escapee.

This chapter explored the daring men and women who defied the confines of their cells, risking everything in their attempts to escape. For most inmates, even unsuccessful bids for freedom ultimately led to a day when their sentences were served, and they walked free. However, not all prisoners shared this fate. The next chapter uncovers stories of those who would never see the outside world again: the executed.

CHAPTER 6

EXECUTIONS

Of all the prisoners that Newcastle Prison held in its almost 100-year history, none drew more public interest than those sentenced to death. The cases of the capitally condemned attracted wide press coverage and public curiosity. From the first crime reports, through the trial and eventually to the execution, newspapers reported the thoughts and behaviours of the condemned men and women to meet the public's seemingly insatiable appetite for information. Nowhere was this public fascination more apparent than on the day of an execution, when the streets surrounding the Gaol would be crammed with people (sometimes in their tens of thousands) hoping to gain a glimpse of the condemned or the hangman. This chapter discusses these executions and how their staging changed across the lifetime of the Prison and sheds light on some of the key figures involved.

Crimes & Causes

The building of the Gaol coincided with a decade of substantial legal reform in England that led to a drastic reduction in the number of crimes punishable by death. At its peak the law of England and Wales included some 220 crimes punishable by death (this series of laws became known as the 'Bloody Code'), but from the late 1830s onwards there was a dramatic reduction in the number of crimes that carried the death sentence and, in reality, only murder was punished by death. Post-mortem punishments included dissection by the Barber Surgeons, ended by the Anatomy Act 1832, and gibbeting, abolished by the Hanging in Chains Act 1834. These brutal relics of an earlier approach to punishment were replaced by burial behind the prison wall, a punishment in and of itself, as we shall see in the following chapter.

Between its opening in 1828 and closure in 1925, 16 prisoners in Newcastle Prison were executed (15 men and one woman - see appendix). They had each been found guilty of murder. The punishment mandated by the law was hanging by the neck until dead, undertaken on wooden gallows, the style of which changed several times in the gaol's lifetime. The youngest prisoner to be hanged was George Vass aged 19, (executed on 14 March 1863) and the oldest John Miller aged 67, (7 December 1901). In 12 of the 16 cases, the convicted prisoner was either related to the murder victim or in a relationship with them: most victims were women. In nearly all cases the prisoners were from the labouring classes, (hawkers, shoemakers, barmen and several former and active military men). One common factor in the murders was the influence of drink, something remarked on at the time in newspapers and in ballads. One ballad, from the execution of Patrick Forbes in 1850 concluded,

> You drunkard's who have families,
> I pray a warning take,
> And strive to rule your passion,
> Before it is too late.
>
> For those who keep up drinking,
> And by Satan led to crime
> Is sure to meet some awful
> And die before their time.

Whilst some cases passed with little comment, some attracted national attention and were the subject of books and radio plays. Most well-known amongst these was the prosecution and eventual execution of John Alexander Dickman in 1910. Dickman had been charged with the murder of John Innes Nisbet on a train travelling between Newcastle and Alnmouth station on 18 March 1910. Nisbet was carrying the wages for a local colliery and his body was found under a seat in one of the train carriages: the money was missing. The murder caused serious alarm, and there was doubt that the right man had been caught. It has been the subject of numerous reinvestigations, including the BBC's *Murder, Mystery* and *My Family*, and it featured on *The Black Museum* radio show, narrated by Orson Welles.

Coverage in The Illustrated Police News of the trial of John Alexander Dickman.

The First Execution: Jane Jamieson

The first prisoner from Newcastle Gaol to die on the gallows was Jane Jamieson (sometimes recorded as Jameson) in 1829. She was the last woman hanged in Newcastle and suffered the further ignominy of being the last criminal to be publicly dissected, an additional punishment for murder until 1832. It may be for these reasons that she has had such a lasting presence in the histories of Newcastle and, if some reports are to be believed, still does.

A sketch of Jane Jamieson at her trial.

Jane Jamieson was a fish hawker who plied her trade in and around the Newcastle Quayside. Her mother, Margaret, was a resident of the Keelmen's Hospital on the New Road (an almshouse established in 1701 for poor keelmen and their widows – it still stands on City Road). In the early hours of 1 January 1829, a keelman, William Ellison (known as Bill or Billy Elley and according to some reports Jane's occasional lover) arrived at Margaret Jamieson's home with a bottle of rum which he shared with the two women to see in the New Year. The following day,

The Keelmen's Hospital.

around 2pm, residents of the Keelmen's Hospital heard an argument between Jamieson and her mother. In evidence given at her trial, Ann Hutchinson (a daughter of one of Margaret's neighbours) claimed that she heard the women angrily arguing, reporting that Jane called Margaret an 'old lousy, stone naked kill-goodman b-----r.' to which her mother replied, 'No, you whore, I did not kill my man, but you killed your two bairns.' The next reported noises were of a distressed cry of, 'Oh my mother!' On entering the room neighbours found Margaret bleeding from a wound in her chest, seemingly inflicted by a poker found near the fire.

Despite the severity of the wound Margaret did not die immediately, but over the next ten days her health dramatically deteriorated, and, despite the efforts of several surgeons, she died on 12 January. Initially there was no criminal investigation, but in the days between the infliction of the wound and her death, numerous rumours spread as to the nature of her demise, with word getting round that she had been murdered. This was complicated by conflicting reports from both mother and daughter. In the immediate aftermath of the attack Jamieson, when questioned by a neighbour, claimed that 'I did not kill my mother, Billy Elley killed my mother.' She said that he had kicked her mother in the chest and the wound was owing to the force with which the 'neb of his shoe' had hit her. At the trial, numerous witnesses noted that Margaret had said that 'Jin had done it with a poker.'

As Margaret's health worsened her story changed. Soon both women claimed that Margaret had been teasing oakum by the fire and fainted from the heat, landing on the poker. We cannot know why her account altered but it would seem that, despite the viciousness of the attack, Margaret had realised the potential deadly consequences for her daughter of being suspected of murder and tried to concoct an alibi that might save her. It was not to be: numerous medical men who visited the patient and the scene attested to the unlikelihood of such a wound being inflicted by anything other than force. Bill Elley could account for his whereabouts and witnesses confirmed that he had not been there at the time of the attack.

Jane Jamieson's trial took place on 5 March 1829 and attracted great public interest. Newcastle's Guildhall was crowded in every available corner. After seven hours of evidence and 25-minutes of deliberation by the jury, Jamieson was found guilty of her mother's murder. The judge, Mr Justice Bailey, pronounced that,

'the sentence of the court is that you be taken to the place from whence you came, and from thence on Saturday morning next, to a place of execution, there to be hanged by the neck till you are dead, your body afterwards to be given for dissection: and May God have mercy on your soul.'

One of the many ironies was that Jamieson was likely familiar with the Guildhall, as the Fish Market, where she worked, had been relocated in 1826 from the Sandhill to the colonnades on its ground floor. Three years later her fate would be sealed in the courtroom above where she sold fish.

As was often the case in murder trials in Newcastle, alcohol played a major part in the Jamieson case. Records indicate that both women had a tendency to drink, which was noted as the cause of Jane Jamieson's downfall, both spiritually and physically. A contemporary report details that,

'she was formerly a smart, clean, good-looking woman; but lately she has been little less than an object of disgust. She had given herself up to the most dissipated habits and appeared to be in the full enjoyment of all their deplorable consequences.'

The Old Fish Market, Sandhill, Newcastle.

In John Sykes' *History of Newcastle* (1833) he described Jamieson in similarly derogatory terms as 'a most disgusting and abandoned female, of most masculine appearance, generally in a state of half nudity.' He detailed her clothing at trial, to emphasise her normal state of degradation, 'she perhaps never was so decently dressed as when upon her trial, having on at that time a black gown, black hat and green shawl.'

The execution was set for Saturday 7 March and on that morning an estimated 20,000 people were on the Town Moor (a large expanse of open land to the north west of the city) to witness it. Over half of those present were reported to be women. Many thousands more lined the streets. This was, no doubt, in part owing to the rarity of seeing a woman executed. The last women to have suffered that fate were Eleanor and Jane Clark in 1789 (prisoners of Northumberland - hanged outside the Westgate Walls).

Map of 1769 showing the site of the gallows on the Town Moor.

After being administered to by the Reverend R Green, the Gaol chaplain, Jamieson was processed from her cell, through the main streets of the town, to the site of the gallows on the Town Moor, north west of the army barracks (close to where BBC Newcastle is today). She sat on top of her coffin in an open cart, and, to block out the watching crowds, she closed her eyes for the 45 minutes it took to travel to the execution site. The procession was an impressive display of local power with Jane's cart led by the Town Sergeants on horseback (in black with cocked hats and carrying ceremonial swords), with eighteen men guarding the cart.

She was placed on a stool on the back of the cart, under the gallows. With the noose around her neck, she uttered the words 'I am ready' and the cart drew away. In the words of contemporary broadsides, Jamieson was 'launched into eternity'. Records show that the execution and procession cost £28 3s 3d, £3 - 3 shillings of which was paid to the executioner. As was customary, her body was left to hang for an hour and then it was taken in procession to the Barber Surgeons' Hall for public dissection. The clothed body was put on public display in the grand entrance to the Hall until 6pm.

The ongoing public interest and fascination with Jamieson after her death can be seen in the numerous ballads and songs about her and her crime and execution that survive from the period. Perhaps the most famous is the Sandgate Pant, recalling how Jamieson's ghost haunts the Pant (a water fountain that stood on the Milk Market). In the ballad Jane is often spotted by drunken boatmen and keelmen selling her wares and lamenting her cruel fate.

The Pant in Sandgate can be seen in the background of this 1890s photograph.

In contrast to Jamieson's public execution and the pageantry surrounding it, the final hangings at Newcastle Prison were a private affair, as we will see, but to understand why this was the case we need to know what led to that change in the intervening years.

The Problem of the Crowd

During the early years of the Gaol, significant changes to capital punishment accompanied broader legal reforms, reducing its application and altering the way it was carried out. The most fundamental change came with the removal of execution from public view. The Capital Punishment (Amendment) Act 1868 legislated that 'judgment of death to be executed on any prisoner … shall be carried into effect within the walls of the prison.' What had once been a public spectacle, with tens of thousands of people watching the last moments of convicted murderers, became a private event witnessed by a select few officials. As such the experiences of Jane Jamieson (the first prisoner from Newcastle Gaol to be hanged, 1829) and Ambrose Quinn (the last, 1919) were dramatically different.

The vast crowds at Jane Jamieson's execution were not unusual - such crowds were commonplace for eighteenth and early nineteenth century executions. However, in the lifetime of the Gaol the management and behaviour of the crowd became the subject of public debate and caused problems for the prison authorities. Of the 16 prisoners executed at Newcastle Gaol the vast majority were hanged inside the walls: only Jane Jamieson (1829), and Mark Sherwood (1844), were hanged on the Town Moor. Between these two executions the debate shifted about the suitability of public executions and processions to watch someone die. The shift can be seen by the fact that Sherwood's execution had been originally planned to take place on the exterior wall of the prison, removing the spectacle of a public procession, but a large and fatal crowd crush at an execution in Nottingham (William Saville, August 1844) led to last minute adjustments and a change of location. Reporting on the decision the *Newcastle Courant* noted that,

'The sad occurrence which was lately witnessed at Nottingham… has caused the idea to be given up of carrying the sentence of the law into effect upon Sherwood in the immediate vicinity in the gaol, as it is feared some serious accident might happen (as at Nottingham) from the want of space to hold the vast multitudes who usually attend such occasions.'

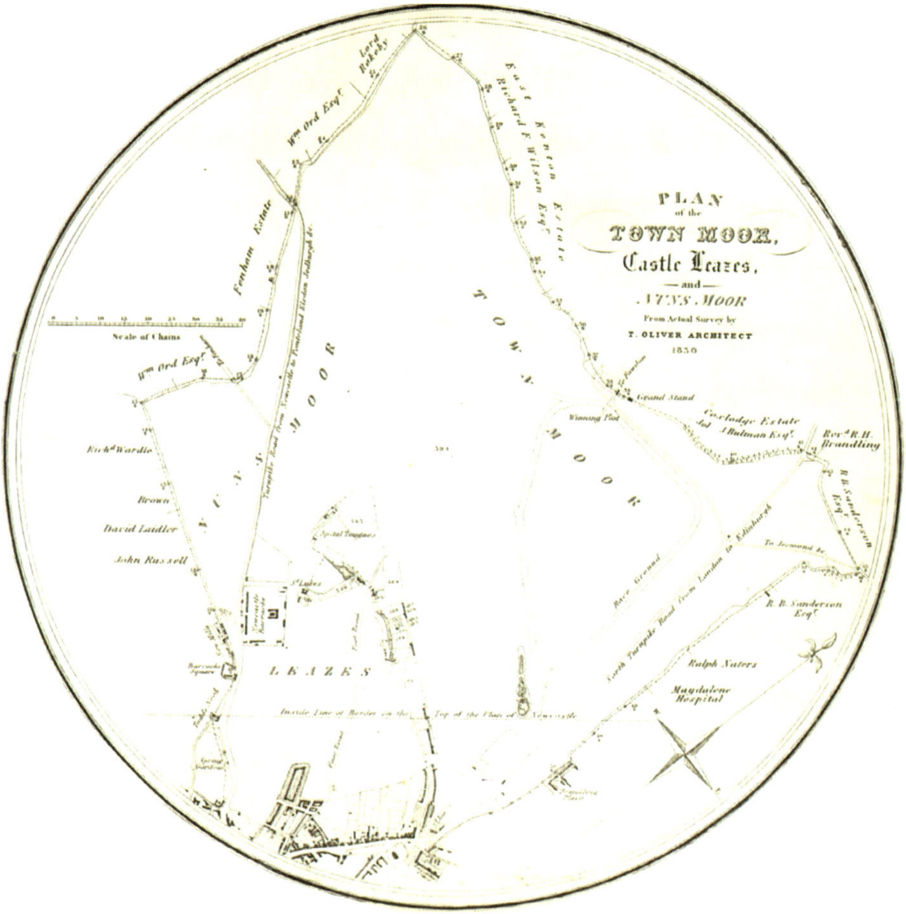

Top: Oliver's 1830 map of the Town Moor showing the Race Ground where an execution took place in 1844, and (above) the Grand Stand on the Course.

Sherwood's execution ultimately took place at the Town Moor Racecourse. Its public nature sparked considerable debate within the Town Council in 1844, leading to a decision that future executions would be conducted against the prison walls. One of the councillors, Alderman Armorer Donkin, stated,

'I cannot conceive anything more horrible than taking a man from prison, parading him through the streets up to the Town Moor, and then hanging him like a dog... Moral Effect! Why more picking of pockets takes place at the foot of the gallows than anywhere else in ten times as many days or weeks in the year.'

RICHARD LOWRY

One thing we know comparatively little about is who attended executions and what they thought about what they had witnessed. Charles Dickens frequently attended executions in London, but accounts of regional executions are vanishingly rare. Luckily, in Newcastle we have the surviving diaries of Richard Lowry – a frequent attendee. Lowry was a Railway Clerk and an educated man. He was present at Mark Sherwood's hanging in 1844 and was only a few yards from the gallows. Remarkably, Lowry seemed most interested in the shape of Sherwood's skull as he was a keen phrenologist - a fascination he shared with many people in Newcastle in this period.

Despite this growing opposition, Newcastle moved comparatively late to locating executions outside, or on, the prison walls. In London, the gallows were relocated from the open land of Tyburn to the external walls of Newgate prison in 1783 and in nearby Durham the first extramural execution took place in 1816. By comparison, the first execution to take place at Newcastle prison was not until 1850. The first man executed on the new gallows was Patrick Forbes. Forbes was an Irish labourer convicted of the murder of his wife, Elizabeth. Much debate ensued about where the execution should take place. When the prison was built there was no provision made for a gallows. Eventually, it was decided that a gallows would be erected against the exterior north wall of the prison. In an astonishing move the decision was made to breach the prison wall from which the prisoner would emerge. Fears of an unpredictable crowd meant that this was deemed safer than processing the prisoner from the entrance gates to the gallows. With Forbes' execution set for Saturday 24 August, stonemasons arrived on the preceding Thursday and undertook the task of breaking a hole large enough to accommodate the prisoner in the prison walls. The authorities were right to be fearful as numerous reports of the execution estimated the crowd on the day at 20,000. The *Newcastle Journal* noted:

'The composition of this crowd will be perfectly well understood by newspaper readers. Vast numbers were of that class which, in all large towns, delight in 'the horrible,' many were females of doubtful character, and not a few were recognised by the police as notorious pickpockets who doubtless plied their vocation as well as they could. Of course, no salutary impression, but the very reverse, could be produced on such parties by witnessing an exhibition so brutal and revolting.'

The *Newcastle Guardian* carried a similarly damning report and hoped that the execution would be the last of its kind in Newcastle,

'This morning... the blood of an unhappy criminal will have been shed... Happily such a spectacle, never exhibited except in cases of premeditated murder, is exceedingly rare in this town... We hope that Newcastle will be spared again from witnessing a Saturnalia of blood.'

In fact, the last execution to take place in public view was that of George Vass in March 1863. Vass was found guilty of the murder of Margaret Docherty – a crime which the presiding Judge, Mr

Baron Martin, declared one of the most revolting he had ever come across. Unlike at the execution of Forbes, the authorities decided to remove Vass entirely from interacting with the crowd and set the execution inside the top walls of the prison, in the south west corner. Although still technically visible to the gathered public it was as close to a private execution as possible. One newspaper reported that 'nothing is visible from the street but the beam of the scaffold.'

In the period between Vass's execution and the next (John William Anderson, 1875) the law changed, dictating that all executions must take place behind the prison walls. From then on, all executions in Newcastle, as elsewhere in the country, took place out of public sight and were witnessed by a small number of state, prison and religious officials. In the later part of the 19th century a purpose-built execution shed was added to the Gaol, and we have the following description from the reports of the execution of William Row(e) (12 March 1890), for the murder of Lily McClarence Wilson.

An engraving of condemned prisoner George Vass in his cell in 1863.

'The drop is always kept in working order, and is quite large enough to admit of a double or even a triple execution. When not in use, the shed is employed as a deadhouse. Screens have been put up to prevent anyone observing the procession from any of the adjacent buildings, but as the execution takes place within a covered shed, it is impossible to see the actual execution from any point, even if a free view could be obtained.'

The only indications that the grim task had been undertaken was a notice on the external walls of the prison, confirming that the death sentence had been carried out, and the raising of a black flag above the prison walls. Despite, or perhaps because of this, the fascination to see any part of the proceedings was intense and in numerous instances reporters, spectators and children were spotted on neighbouring roofs and other vantage points attempting to gain a glimpse. At the execution of Samuel George Emery (1894), for the murder of Mary Ann Marshall, the *Newcastle Courant* remarked that the crowd was 'not to such an extent as had been noted on previous occasions' but there was clearly still great interest - the paper providing a very evocative description of the scene outside the prison.

'The men smoked, the women smoked, the women talked, and the children, unfortunately a numerous section of the bystanders, listened with ears pricked and keen eyes to the discussions which were heard here and there in the groups as the daylight slowly asserted itself, bringing into sterner and even more gloomy relief than before the black walls and roof of the prison building.'

As Emery's execution showed, the appetite of the crowds for the spectacle of capital punishment had not diminished, despite the only signs of the deed's completion being a 'black flag waving in the breeze.' What is clear, is that a once public event intended to display the power of the criminal justice system was, by the end of the Prison's lifetime a private and almost hermetically sealed event. This can be seen in the last two executions.

The Final Executions

On the morning of Wednesday 26 November 1919 two men (Ambrose Quinn and Ernest Bernard Scott) were executed at Newcastle Prison. They were the last two people to suffer that fate in Newcastle and, although unconnected, their crimes and personal profiles bore many similarities.

Ambrose Quinn (left) and Ernest Bernard Scott were both executed at Newcastle Prison on the same day in November 1919.

Scott and Quinn were both 28 years of age at the time of their executions and had served, respectively, as a fireman and a mechanic in the Royal Air Force. Both men were charged with the murder of their partners, in Scott's case his sweetheart Rebecca Jane Quinn and in Ambrose's case his wife, Elizabeth Ann Quinn (although the victims shared a surname they were not related). The crimes were strikingly similar, a fact that did not go unnoticed by the press. One newspaper observed that:

'[The crimes] occurred within two days of each other, were committed by men of the same age, both were due to jealousy, both took place in the open air. In both instances a razor was used and was used in the same way… and in both cases there were witnesses, so that there was no doubt as to who committed the crime.'

The Illustrated Police News depicts the murder charge against a Northumberland miner in August 1919.

Although there were similarities between the two men and the crimes for which they were to be punished, their behaviour whilst awaiting their fates could not have been more different. Reports in the local press detailed Scott's unshakeable and seemingly unmoved countenance until his execution. The *Illustrated Police News* carried a report and accompanying illustration of the crime, including the detail that whilst in prison Scott 'spent his time singing, whistling and humming hymn tunes.' One prison officer told the journalist that he had met six men prior to their executions during his career but had, 'never seen anyone display such extraordinary calm' as Scott.

Whilst incarcerated, Scott wrote prolifically to family and friends, including several letters to Rebecca Quinn's parents, although they refused to accept them. During visits from family members, he was reported using 'gallows humour.' The *Blyth News*, reporting a visit Scott had from his brother, reported the condemned man as joking, "This is a good Government. They are very kind. Do you notice my new suit? But see how low it is round the neck. You know what that is for!"

In contrast, from the limited detail available, it is clear that Quinn was in considerable distress in the prison. In one remarkable report a journalist wrote of a meeting with Scott in which he was claimed to have said (on hearing Quinn crying) 'Do you hear him?; he has been at that for a fortnight. I have been constantly singing to cheer him up, but it's no use!'

The jury that found Quinn guilty had recommended him for mercy (a not uncommon practice) and despite caution from Quinn's solicitor, there was a widespread public belief that he would be granted a reprieve. One report noted how the Lord Mayor of Newcastle (Walter Lee) sent a personal telegram to the Home Office conveying the strength of public sentiment that Quinn should be reprieved. However, despite the efforts of petitioners, the Home Office refused the request, and the execution of both men was set for the morning of Wednesday 26 November. Scott was to be hanged at 8am and Quinn at 9.15am.

Scott refused to be represented by counsel at his trial and, although witness after witness gave evidence pointing to Scott's guilt, he asked them no questions, nor did he address the jury in his own defence. When asked by the judge whether he had any statement to make as to why the death sentence should not be passed, Scott replied, "Not in the least! I will get the happiness I want then. I have long looked for it and was deprived of it. I will not be deprived of it in the next world."

Double executions were a rare event in Newcastle. The most recent occurred in 1901, when John Miller and John Robert Miller were hanged for the murder of John Ferguson. Before that, such an event had not taken place since the 18th century. In a curious twist, the hangman who executed Quinn and Scott was John Ellis: his first role as an executioner's assistant had been at the Millers' hanging in 1901.

Reports noted that, despite miserable weather, a sizeable crowd was in attendance in the streets surrounding the prison from dawn. There were reports of gatherings on the nearby City Road bridge, with several horses and carriages reportedly having pulled up prior to 8 am. The newspapers believed this was to try and get a glimpse of the black flag that had previously been raised following an execution (a practice, in fact, ended in 1902). By the time of Quinn's execution, the crowd had a younger composition, with one newspaper reporting that it believed it was, in part, made up of several children on their way to school - they were most likely to have been on their way to the Jubilee School which was directly behind the prison.

Ultimately, the waiting crowd for both executions were left disappointed as no visible signs of the execution could be seen. One newspaper reported that 'no bell was tolled and no flag was exhibited. The prison bell did not even strike the hour of eight.' The solemnity and secrecy with which this double execution took place was in marked contrast to the last public execution at the Gaol in 1863. There was merely a slight commotion minutes after Quinn's execution, one newspaper recording that,

'three separate crashes of glass were heard. The crowd outside the prison concluded that some of the prisoners had broken their cell-windows by way of a demonstration, but enquiries showed that the noise was made by some workmen engaged within the prison.'

Both men were said to have met their fate with bravery and minimal fuss. Reports noting that the men made no final statements and submitted to the regulation pinioning (tying of wrists and ankles) with no trouble. At the coroner's inquest that followed their deaths the reports noted that Quinn was 5 feet 5 [1.65 metres] and weighed 137 lbs [62 kg]. His 'drop' was recorded as 7 feet 10 inches [2.4 metres]. Scott (5 ft 5 ½ ins [1.66 metres] and 151 lbs [68.5 kg]) was given a slightly shorter 'drop' of 7 feet 3 inches [2.21 metres]. After hanging for the customary hour, their bodies were buried in the Prison yard.

A STARTLING SUICIDE IN 1911

For some prisoners facing the punishment of death by hanging, the fear was too much to bear. Alexander Ingram, 27, took his own life in prison. Charged with the murder of his wife and two stepchildren, he slipped the guards when leaving his cell at Newcastle Prison and jumped over the railings to his death. Public sympathy did not extend to this tragic figure though as, at his burial at Heaton Cemetery, vast crowds turned out to boo the coffin procession and even tried to storm the gates– requiring police to hold them back.

The Hangmen

Throughout the Prison's history, despite changes in the staging of executions, one aspect remained unchanged: the role of the hangman. For centuries, the position of executioner was largely informal, with the task sometimes carried out by fellow prisoners in exchange for leniency in their own sentences. It was a widely despised role and there are numerous instances across Europe of hangmen living as social outcasts. However, from the mid-nineteenth century onwards, the role was steadily professionalised and it grew in stature, with the hangman no longer a reviled figure but instead a minor 'celebrity' with a sought after public position.

By the mid-19th century hangmen from York or Scotland were employed to carry out executions in the North East, such as the 1865 execution of Matthew Atkinson at Durham (undertaken by York's hangman Thomas Askern). Askern's bungling of the Atkinson execution (the rope broke and Atkinson had to be hauled up and hanged again) was met with curses from the crowd and questions in the House of Commons. Subsequent reports noted that such was the anger of the crowd that Askern feared returning to the region.

After 1868, when executions were moved behind prison walls, the hangman became a more elusive and, consequently, more intriguing figure to the public. Over time, hangmen like William Marwood introduced innovative techniques, most notably the 'long drop' - a method designed to break the neck instantly and prevent prolonged strangulation. Marwood's innovations helped professionalise the role and he was arguably the first to gain celebrity status - such was his renown that people would attend the Dun Cow Inn in Durham (Marwood's lodgings for Durham Prison executions) the night before a hanging as he was known to regale a willing audience with tales of his work.

Testament to the fascination around hangmen and their increasing celebrity status can be seen in executioner James

Executioner James Berry gained celebrity status in the late 19th century.

Berry's recording of his travel plans for the 1886 execution of Patrick Judge at Newcastle (on 16 November 1886). Recalling his tactics for avoiding expectant crowds he detailed how he would take a different train from that originally booked, to avoid being disturbed on his journey. Similarly, he would change trains at the nearest local station and take a branch line train to his destination. Leaving the prison and returning home was often difficult, as crowds would gather to wait for him after an execution, as was the case following Patrick Judge's execution.

Patrick Judge had been sentenced to death for the murder of his wife, Jane, and the case aroused much local interest. The streets surrounding the prison, most notably Worswick Street, were packed with people as it afforded the best view of the black flag. Such was the intrigue around the hanging that the execution was temporarily halted when a prison warder spotted three men sitting on top of the roof of a building overlooking the Prison. Berry was concerned that the men might be relatives of the condemned man and ordered that they be removed, but as the prison officials had no authority over the neighbouring building, it was not within their power. In the end the execution went smoothly but problems arose when Berry tried to leave the prison. Writing of the aftermath of Judge's execution, Berry's diaries recorded the 'big and enthusiastic crowd waiting to see me and my assistant depart.' He was aware that one or two men in the crowd knew him by sight and knew the train by which he was to travel home. The eager mob rushed to the train station and, despite the best efforts of the railway's officials and police, managed to 'burst through the barriers with a howl of exultation and filled the platform.' They were to be disappointed. Berry and his assistant had already travelled over the River Tyne to Gateshead station and booked a train back to Newcastle. On arrival they switched onto the mainline train for Bradford, undetected, and the crowd 'under the firm impression that we had not entered the station.' In just over a century the hangman had gone from a vilified figure of public fury to a star attraction for the morbidly curious.

Who Would be a Hangman?

Finally, it should not be forgotten that the hangmen were often as terrified as the prisoners they were about to dispatch. At the double execution of John Miller and John Robert Miller in 1901, the executioner James Billington was assisted by a young John Ellis, attending his first hanging. The younger Miller had been removed from the condemned cells to the prison's hospital owing to his increasingly erratic behaviour. Such was the concern over Miller's mental health, there was correspondence between the prison doctor and Home Office to confirm he was in a fit state to be executed. Originally planned as a double execution, the undersheriff wrote to the Home Office indicating that JR Miller's behaviour may necessitate separate hangings.

'Apart from the fact the building in HM Prison here set apart for the purpose of the execution is somewhat circumscribed in space, the struggle and cries of the younger man, with which it seems

The Millers during their trial.

probable the executioner will have to contend, will doubtless affect the older prisoner, and the execution be thus rendered exceptionally difficult'.

The undersheriff's reservations were heeded and a late decision was made to separate the executions by 90 minutes. This did nothing to calm the mind of young Miller and Ellis recorded his terror at the experience of spending the night in the same prison as him.

'My bedroom was on the same floor as the hospital, and young Miller's screams and cries kept me awake most of the night. I lay on my back staring into darkness. This was my first execution – was it always going to be like this I wondered?'.

Ellis carried out many more executions and returned to Newcastle to oversee the execution of John Alexander Dickman in 1910. Dickman was the only prisoner Ellis granted a last dying request, despite disliking him.

'The only last request I didn't refuse on the scaffold came from John Dickman, the Newcastle train murderer, another man with

The crowd outside the Prison at Dickman's execution in 1910.

an ugly gleam in his eye during his last few moments on earth. Less than a minute before I executed him Dickman demanded rather than requested to be hanged in his shirt sleeves, and although his arms were already pinioned, I decided to let him have his own way'.

Ellis feared that refusing Dickman the request to remove his coat, as he was in 'such an ugly mood', may have 'precipitated a scene.'

DICKMAN'S PIGEON

There were many superstitions surrounding the gallows, but one curious story was relayed in the press shortly after Alexander John Dickman's hanging in 1910. The first time the doomed man stepped into the yard for his exercise, following his transference to the condemned cell, a pigeon flew down and landed close to him. The bird came again the next day, and the next—each time Dickman took his walk the bird appeared. Then on the day before his execution the prisoner came out into the prison yard and looked for the bird. But it did not come. Presently the warders said the time allowed for exercise had come to an end, but Dickman pleaded with them let him stay outside a little longer. The gaolers yielded, and Dickman walked the yard for another hour. Then, having been abandoned by the little bird, Dickman said this was an omen that he was meant to die, and turned his steps towards his cell. He later found out his appeal had failed.

Conclusion

In a short period, executions at Newcastle Prison underwent significant changes, yet one constant remained: a prisoner left hanging at the end of a rope. Despite the horror and intrigue surrounding executions during this time, what often troubled prisoners more than their impending death on the gallows was the fate of their burial. The nature and location of their final resting place caused them greater distress than the thought of the hanging itself, and as we will see, often for good reason. It is to this final punishment that we now turn.

CHAPTER 7

BURIAL & POST-MORTEM PUNISHMENT

At 10am on the morning of 12 October 1925, Robert Stuart, Medical officer for Newcastle Prison, and Colonel HMA Hales, the Governor of Durham Prison, were ushered inside the walls of Newcastle gaol where they were met with an astonishing scene. In front of them were a series of plain wooden coffins containing the bodies of the men executed and buried during the lifetime of the gaol. The coffins had been exhumed by two local grave diggers, but remained unopened, and Hales and Stuart faced the grim task of examining their contents. The results of their investigations, which were reported nationally, caused a great stir and had lasting implications for the treatment of criminal bodies. In this chapter, we will explore why the prisoners were buried there and uncover the often-overlooked post-mortem punishments that accompanied a capital sentence.

Post-Mortem Punishment

As late as the twentieth century, in England, there could be punishments meted out to prisoners after death. These were referred to as post-mortem punishments and were reserved for the most heinous crimes. The most common 'additional' punishments, dictated by the Murder Act 1751, were public dissection (carried out by surgeons, often in front of a paying audience) and gibbeting (where the executed body was encaged in iron and suspended from a wooden mast, commonly erected near the site of the crime). The horror of post-mortem punishments was enhanced by the denial of a Christian burial and the refusal of the authorities to release the body for interment. Indeed, throughout the lifetime of the Gaol, all but one of the executed prisoners were buried behind the prison walls, with only their initials marked on the nearest wall to indicate the location of their grave.

Traditionally, in Newcastle, executed prisoners were buried in the unconsecrated north side of the graveyard of St Andrew's Church, adjacent to the original town gaol at Newgate. Northumberland

County prisoners were interred at nearby St John's Church. The burial of criminal bodies on the north side of churchyards was common practice. It was also the occasional resting place for excommunicates, unbaptized infants, some who had taken their own lives through suicide and, in the case of St Andrew's, several women, and one man, hanged for witchcraft in 1650. This practice led many families, by the late eighteenth century, to view the north side of a graveyard as 'polluted.' This seemingly defiled graveyard was never used for prisoners from Newcastle Gaol, but in many cases their fate was arguably worse.

St. Andrew's Parish Church.

Executed prisoners were buried in the north side of St Andrew's Church.

THE MURDER ACT 1751

The Murder Act 1751 stated that 'for better preventing the horrid crime of murder... some further terror and peculiar mark of infamy be added to the punishment.' It was introduced, in part, owing to a perceived crime wave in mid-century London. In the same year it was enacted, William Hogarth produced a four-part series of engravings entitled, 'The Four Stages Of Cruelty'. In the final plate of this morally instructive series, detailing the life of Tom Nero, Nero is seen on the dissection table, following his execution at Tyburn, and his organs are being eaten by the dog whom he was torturing in the first plate of the series.

Dissection of Jane Jamieson and the Barber Surgeons

We know from reports of executions in Newcastle that sometimes, in the minds of the condemned, the fear of post-mortem punishment, particularly indecent burial, was more potent than hanging. In 1829 one broadside recorded Jane Jamieson's last moments before leaving the Gaol en route to the gallows at the Town Moor. It detailed that she asked the attendant minister 'a question about her body' but was told that 'she was not to care about her body but about her soul.' Jamieson had good reason to be fearful as, although her body was not ultimately buried in the prison yard, she became the last person in Newcastle to suffer the additional punishment of public dissection.

Following her execution Jamieson was ordered to suffer 'some further terror and peculiar mark of infamy' – in this case public dissection by the Barber Surgeons. Her body was processed in the coffin she had sat upon on the journey to the execution, to the Barber Surgeon's Hall in nearby Manors. The hall was a grand building located in what is now known as the East Pilgrim Street area, but in the nineteenth century was next to the Holy Jesus Hospital (still standing today).

The Barber Surgeon's Hall.

The best description of the Barber Surgeons' Hall was written by a visitor in 1697,

'within a pretty garden walled in, full of flowers and greens in potts and in the Borders; its a good neate building of Brick. There I saw the roome with a round table in it railed round with seates or Benches for ye Conveniency in their dissecting and anatomising a body, and reading Lectures on all parts. There were two bodyes that had been anatomised one the bones were fastned with wires the other had had the flesh boiled off and so some of ye Ligeament remained and dryed with it, and so the parts were held together by its own muscles and sinews that were dryed with it. Over this was another roome in wch was the skin of a man that was taken off after he was dead, and dressed, and so was stuffed- the body and limbs. It Look'd and felt like a sort of parchment. In this roome I could take a viewe of the whole town, it standing on high ground, and a pretty Lofty building.'

Upon arrival, Jamieson's clothed body was put on public display in the grand entrance until 6pm. In the two weeks that followed, ticketed lectures were given on the dissection of her brain and body by John Fife (surgeon and founder of the medical school and, later, Mayor of Newcastle). The sessions were free to attend for medical men and members of the public could observe, for a small fee (10s 6d for the 2-week course and 2s 6d for a single lecture).

The lectures were attended by an apprentice surgeon, Thomas Giordani Wright, who noted in his diaries that, 'they may be very useful to the tyros of the profession and highly interesting to a general audience, but they do not contain any information as anatomical lectures.' He added that Fife's 'manner of delivery is so deliberate and slow that the whole of his orating... might easily be compressed into one third or a quarter of the time it occupies.' One thing that did impress Wright was the 'freshness' of Jamieson's brain, which he said was a rarity in anatomical demonstration – testament to the state of many of the bodies provided to surgeons from the illicit trade of grave robbery.

SIR JOHN FIFE (1795 - 1871)

John Fife was an accomplished surgeon working in Newcastle in the nineteenth century. Amongst his many medical roles he was Senior Surgeon at the Newcastle Infirmary and also operated at the Barber Surgeons at Manors. He took an active role in founding the Newcastle School of Medicine and alongside his surgical career he was also very politically active. Fife was twice Mayor of Newcastle and was knighted in 1840 for his courage in suppressing a Chartist outbreak in 1839. Fife was also a committed phrenologist and one of the founding members of the Newcastle Phrenological Society. His brother, George, was Surgeon to Newcastle Gaol when leading Scottish Phrenologist, George Combe, was allowed into the gaol in 1835 to examine the heads of some of the prisoners.

Until recently it was not known where, or even if, Jamieson's body was buried. From surviving archival records we know that it was not unheard of for the Barber Surgeons to gift the bones of the executed to colleagues, as was the case at the dissection of Dorothy Gatenby (or Gatinby) in 1754. Even more disturbingly, following the 1817 execution of Charles Smith, a grim relic appeared that is preserved by Newcastle Library. A year after Smith's public dissection the following detail appeared in the Durham County Advertiser,

'Literary relic – An eminent collector and Antiquarian of Newcastle is possessed of a piece of the skin of the late Charles Smith, executed near the town last year for the murder of Charles Stewart, which he had washed, tanned and dressed for the purposes of binding a large paper copy of the murderer's dying speech!!!'

The Particulars of the Trial and Execution of Charles Smith by John W Bell, which may contain a piece of Smith's skin.

In Smith's case, a portion of his skin was included as a page in a book owned by John W Bell, titled T*he Particulars of the Trial and Execution of Charles Smith*. The book contained ephemera from the trial and execution and even, possibly in Bell's hand, a drawing of the devil sat on top of the gallows on the Town Moor. However, Jane Jamieson's body did not ultimately have an ignominious end. One of the discoveries of the Newcastle Gaol project was that Jamieson, once the surgeons had finished with her, was given a public burial at the dissenters' burial ground at Ballast Hills, to the east of the city. This would have been a rare practice, as great efforts were made under the Murder Act to ensure that, 'in no case whatsoever the body of any murderer shall be suffered to be buried.'

Testament to the fascination surrounding the crime can be seen in local antiquarian John Bell's record that, 'a great number of persons assembled to witness the interment.' Bell went on: 'The Remains of this unfortunate woman were interred in the Ballast Hills Ground in the afternoon of Friday Sen'night, the last of the anatomical demonstrations having been concluded on the preceding day.'

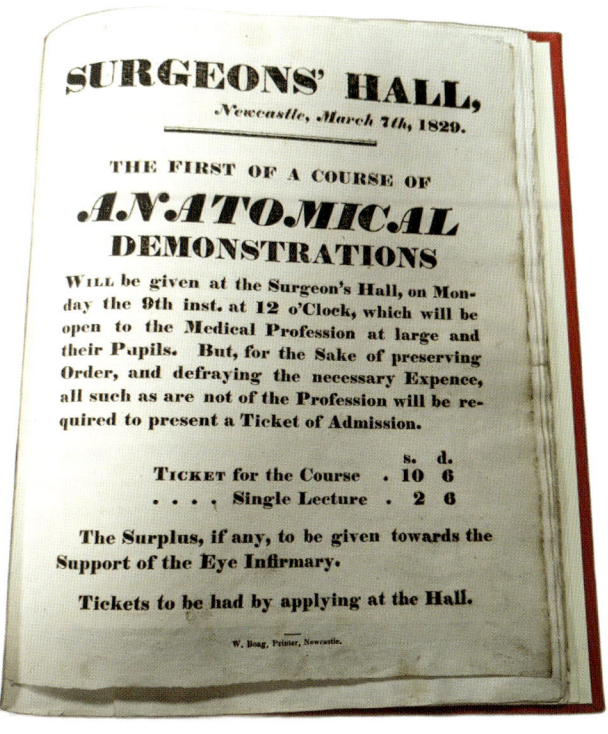

Advert showing the growing fascination with the anatomy of the human body.

Body Snatching and Ballast Hills

Despite her public burial, Jamieson's fears about her body's resting place were well founded. Before the Anatomy Act 1832, the only bodies officially available for dissection, without prior consent, were those of executed criminals. This limited supply meant that body-snatchers, sometimes known as resurrectionists, operated throughout the country in churchyards and cemeteries to dig up newly buried corpses to sell to surgeons. Newcastle was no exception. In January 1829 the *Newcastle Courant* reported the discovery of the body of a 7-year-old girl in a trunk at the Queen's Head Inn. The body was that of Elizabeth Mills, the daughter of a local shoemaker, who had been buried the previous day at Ballast Hills, following her death from burns in Newcastle Infirmary. The newspaper explained that the alarm had been raised owing to the way the trunk was 'corded' and the 'Scotch dialect' of the man who deposited it at the Inn. This is unsurprising as the newspapers had been awash with the, now infamous, Burke and Hare trial in Edinburgh which had begun a matter of weeks before the discovery of the trunk.

Further testament to the fears surrounding body snatching can be seen in the pricing charts for Ballast Hills: a grave of 3s 6d was standard, but a family could pay extra (by the foot) to get a deeper grave up to 10ft [3 metres] (9s 6d). In the same year that Jane Jamieson was buried, a new cemetery at Westgate Hill, opened to provide a respectable burial site for dissenters and the town's poor. In his sermon for the first interment at Westgate the Reverend Pengilly said:

'Everyone who has paid any considerable attention to the former places of interment, whether in reference to the church yards or the burial place at the Ballast Hills, must know, that except in the very small recent enlargements, the portions of the ground so appropriated have been literally crowded with the dead… I have known what it is to witness the bones of a friend… tossed up to the surface to make room for another.'

BURKE AND HARE

Perhaps the most famous of all resurrectionists and body snatchers, were William Burke and William Hare. Burke and Hare supplied Dr Robert Knox's Anatomical School in Edinburgh with bodies, the first of which was a lodger of Hare's who had died still owing him money. In truth, their reputation as body snatchers is somewhat of an anomaly, as they were really men who murdered to supply the anatomical trade. In all they were responsible for at least 16 murders and were eventually caught and tried. Hare turned Kings evidence against Burke and ultimately escaped punishment, but Burke was hanged in front of huge crowds in Edinburgh on 28 January 1829. As an additional punishment his body was subject to public dissection and his skeleton remains on show to this day at The University of Edinburgh's Anatomical Museum. A cruel irony!

William Hare and William Burke

Jamieson's case continued to arouse public fascination long after her death. Commenting on capital punishment in 1851 the *Gateshead Observer* recorded that it was 'not generally known' that the landlord of a 'low tavern in Newcastle' had purchased Jamieson's 'nut-measure' (a small wooden tape measure) following her death and would hire it out as a dice box for a fee. It was not unheard of for people to seek to purchase souvenirs from an execution including clothing and lengths of the hangman's rope.

STEALING OF BODIES
FROM THE
Ballast Hills Burying Ground.

On Saturday morning Nov. 7, 1829, great sensation was excited among the inhabitants in the neighbourhood of the Ballast Hills, by the discovery of a body having been disinterred and stolen from the burying-ground. On Friday afternoon, a young woman was buried, of the name of Hills or Mills, of Berwick-square; and some of these inhuman monsters, who live by the dead, had, in the night of Friday, or Saturday morning, taken up the body, and in the most unfeeling and brutish manner, strewed her grave clothes and coffin about the ground, and carried off the body! every search has been made, so as to detect the depredators—and the different coach offices were applied to, but they could not recollect of any box of a suspicious description, so that the conclusion is, the body must now be in the hands of some of the medical faculty in the town, or have been shipped off to that famed and awful depository of the dead—Edinburgh!—The brutal manner in which this offence has been committed, has exasperated the public, and has excited additional surprise that this burying ground, the most used in the town, should be so neglected; and among other persons, the lodge-keeper has not escaped the tongue of scandal. This is, however, a public burying place, and the persons who receive the fees for interment ought to see to its being in a protected state, and to see, too, that the persons whom they have employed to look after it are not remiss in their duty, for of all the instances of body-stealing that we have had related, this seems to be the most outrageous to the feelings that has ever occured.

Broadside from 1829.

Burial Within the Prison Walls

In the years between Jamieson's execution and the next at Newcastle Gaol, two important pieces of legislation were passed. The Anatomy Act 1832 removed the post-mortem punishment of dissection and the Hanging in Chains Act 1834 removed gibbeting and provided that the bodies of executed prisoners must 'be buried within the Precincts of the Prison in which such Prisoner shall have been confined after Conviction'. As a result 15 of the 16 executed criminals at Newcastle were buried within the walls of the prison and in some cases denied a Christian burial.

After an execution it was customary for the body to hang for one hour, a centuries-old tradition, and then (after 1868) for a coroner's inquest to take place on the body, attended by a jury. The jury's role was to confirm both the cause of death and identity of the deceased. The burial would take place the same day, in the presence of the prison chaplain and officials. A notice of certification was then placed on an external prison wall to publicly confirm that the execution had taken place. In almost all cases of prison burials there was consistency in that the coffin was reported as 'plain' or 'common deal' (an inexpensive pine/fir board) and painted black, in line with the sombre palette applied to the scaffold enclosures. Despite its simple style, the coffin could attract great public interest. In 1863, on the night prior to the last public execution (of George Vass) a dense crowd had gathered outside the prison. When the coffin arrived there was a rush and the *Newcastle Journal* claimed that were it not for the police 'clearing the way' the proceedings would have been greatly delayed. Noting the arrival of the coffin and a small black footstool believed to be for the condemned prisoner the newspaper continued that, 'it is impossible to describe the excitement of the crowd on the arrival of these articles.'

Denying a 'Decent Burial'

Burial behind the prison wall may seem insignificant in comparison to the brutal post-mortem punishment inflicted on Jane Jamieson, but to grasp its significance, we must consider the context of the time. The denial or degradation of proper burial rites had long been a form of punishment for those who violated societal norms. The location, occasion and rites performed were essential elements in a 'proper' or 'decent' burial and the denial or denigration of one or all, was a fate feared by many, including convicted criminals.

The First Prison Burial

In 1844, Mark Sherwood was the first person to be buried within the walls of Newcastle Gaol. At his execution measures were taken to shield his corpse from public view. Unlike the execution of Jamieson, Sherwood was not pulled from a cart but was placed on a specially built raised scaffold platform surrounded by wooden boards, to hide his body from view. Sherwood's coffin was concealed beneath the raised and covered platform on which he was hanged, and his body was lowered into the coffin and then processed back to the prison in a carriage before being interred. At the Gaol his body was placed in a 'simple deal' coffin and this was buried in the 'garden of the gaol' within 'a few feet of the Western Wall which runs from the corner opposite the George the Fourth public house to the railway station.'

Sherwood, like Jamieson, had been concerned about what would happen to his body. Reports of his execution noted that one of his last requests was that

'the grave might be deep, and hoped his remains would not be allowed to be disturbed. He also desired, if not contrary to any legal regulation, that the burial service might be read when he was committed to the earth. In compliance with his wish the grave was made seven feet [2.1 metres] deep, as subsequently stated but the burial service was not read.'

His fears were not unfounded as, despite the *Anatomy Act*, three years before Sherwood's imprisonment Newcastle had been gripped by a body snatching scandal close to the prison.

THE SCANDAL OF SOPHIA QUIN

In 1840 Sophia Quin had died in the house of her daughter, Rosanna Rox, in Clogger's Entry in Sandhill, Newcastle, and was due to be buried at the dissenter's burial ground at Ballast Hills (resting place of Jane Jamieson), to the East of the city. However, the coffin bearers instead took the body straight to the Surgeons' Hall at Manors. When Rosanna was refused entry, she ran to the Mayor's house and raised the alarm. The Mayor, in attendance with Rosanna and a Police Officer, strode down to the Surgeons' Hall and demanded entry. At first the Surgeons refused, but eventually entry was gained and Rosanna saw wood shavings from her mother's coffin on the hall floor, with her torn and tattered clothes discarded under a table. On further

investigation, they lifted the lid of what appeared to be a large chest and found her mother's body sitting upright in warm water up to her shoulders – the sight of which caused Rosanna to faint. This was most likely the anatomists practice of sluicing the corpse, intended to increase the 'safety and longevity' of the body by washing away any harmful bacteria and cooling the body. Sophia Quin's body was recovered and eventually buried, but the episode caused a great scandal in the region and went to trial – the reports of which even made it into the distinguished medical journal, *The Lancet*.

What happened after death preoccupied the final days of condemned prisoners. Prior to his execution in 1850 Patrick Forbes asked to see Alderman Dunn, a visiting magistrate, who had taken an interest in his case. Dunn and Forbes 'walked together in the garden' of the Gaol where Forbes 'pointed out to him the spot in which his body would be laid, observing that he had felt an anxious desire to see the place.'

The locations of burials within the prison yard changed over time and it was not always clear to prisoners where they would be laid to rest. One report of the execution of George Vass, in 1863, detailed that when passing from the pinioning room to the scaffold, the 'mournful procession passed over the site of the grave (of which however they were in ignorance)'. The newspaper noted, 'thus the poor creature unwittingly trod over the very spot of earth where a few hours later his mortal remains were laid for ever.'

The grave was, perhaps understandably, in the thoughts of the those waiting to be executed long into the twentieth century. In the final visit from his wife, John Dickman, despite maintaining his innocence, was reported to have said that he was 'dead to everything now and appeared to be in his tomb speaking to them from beyond the grave.' Similarly, Ernest Bernard Scott composed a poem which ended,

> 'Soon my sorrows will be over.
> Soon my labours will be ended,
> My tongue will cease
> My heart no longer beat
> And in my grave peacefully sleep.'

Despite this final wish, on a cold October morning in 1925, Medical Officer Robert Stuart and Governor Hales stood facing a series of exhumed coffins, amongst them Scott's. In order to find out why, we must look to the efforts involved in the Prison's closure.

Demolition, Desecration & Missing Bodies

Earlier in 1925, HMP Newcastle became the latest local gaol to be closed following an economy drive by the Home Office. The prisoners were moved to the more commodious facilities at Durham and the City Corporation took up an option to purchase the site. Early plans included its total removal to make way for a new principal thoroughfare and a replacement for Newcastle's aging Police Headquarters and Court. However, it was eventually decided to demolish the buildings and build a much-needed telephone exchange on part of the footprint (a building that still stands today). However, in order to carry out the plan, the authorities faced a problem – the reinterment of the bodies of executed criminals buried within the prison walls.

During the lifetime of the Prison, numerous Home Office circulars had been sent detailing the treatment of criminal bodies. The last came in 1922 and stated that the graves of the executed should,

'no longer be distinguished by names, initials, or any other marks on the walls. Such records are undesirable as they perpetuate the memory of the crime, cause unnecessary pain to relatives and rouse a morbid interest in the prisoners.'

It was decided that any marks locating graves must be obliterated, and to facilitate this a map or plan of the current graves should first be submitted by each gaol and a Register of Graves be sent to the Prison Commission. Once these documents had been completed prison governors were to 'effectively obliterate all wall marks, … and report when this had been done'. We know this was undertaken in part, as following the closure of the gaol, photographs appeared in the *Northern Daily Mail* and *Newcastle Chronicle* showing an Inspector viewing one of the stones with the initials crossed out. Another newspaper noted, on a tour of the now closed prison, that, 'those initials have been erased from the stone work … and only the defacement of the slabs of stone now suggest that those slabs had been called upon to serve as headstones for interred persons.'

Despite the Home Office's request for mapping, the location of the bodies became a serious problem for the authorities in Newcastle because they struggled to locate the placement of each grave.

An onlooker observes the defaced stones that had once borne the initials of executed men interred at Newcastle Prison.

The difficulties inherent in locating the bodies can be seen in Medical Officer Stuart's confidential report to the Home Office. Of the 15 graves dug that day, only 11 revealed coffined bodies and in four instances no coffin was found. Reporting on the findings for Mark Sherwood (1844), Patrick Forbes (1850), William Row(e) (1890) and Samuel Emery (1894), Stuart noted: 'at a depth of about 11 feet [3.35 metres], we found no trace of body or coffin.' Sherwood's earlier fears for the safety of his body had been well founded.

Stuart's report provided details of the state of the found bodies, which gives an insight into the changing preparation and treatment of the criminal body over time. In all but two instances, the bodies had been buried in clothes: Alexander Dickman (1910) and William J Cavanagh (1917), had their clothes placed alongside them in the coffin. But perhaps the most astonishing finding was in the grave of Patrick Judge, (1886). Known as the 'Walker Wife Murderer', Judge had lost a leg in an industrial accident, whilst building the Ouseburn bridge. On examining the contents of his coffin Stuart reported: 'There was no trace of lime. The bones were bare; and with the bones there was found a 'bucket' for an artificial leg.'

THE BUCKET LEG

Fig. 40.

The 'bucket' was a government supplied prothesis (often used for military injuries) for amputations above the knee. Its name came from its shape, the bucket incorporating the remaining limb, which then would connect to a 'pin' or 'peg' which took the weight of the person's body. Remarkably, little or no mention is made of Patrick Judge's 'bucket' in reports of his execution in 1886.

The most significant finding was regarding the use of lime/quicklime on the corpses. This discovery had lasting implications for prison burial policy. In several of the graves, lime/quicklime had been sprinkled over the body. It had been used in the coffins of Henry Perkins (1905) onwards. The intention was to be a catalyst for the rapid destruction of the corpse, another indignity in the long history of additional punishments placed on executed men and women. Reporting on the planned efforts to exhume the bodies the *Newcastle Evening Chronicle* stated that, 'executed persons are buried in quick lime, and the supposition is that within a few days after they passed from the scaffold, little is left to suggest that that little was once a human body'.

However, far from destroying the body, Stuart reported that the lime had had a preservative effect. Stuart commended the fortitude of the gravediggers as the stench proceeding from the preserved remains was 'of such a degree, that it could hardly be described.' Writing in support of Medical Officer Stuart's findings, Governor Hale recorded that 'the stench from bodies buried as long as 15 years ago…could scarcely be endured.' Adding the stomach-churning detail that, 'it was obvious from the fetid slushy pickle of rotten humanity that was exposed to view on exhumation that quicklime acts as a preservative of muscle, flesh, viscera and bones.' In line with Medical Officer Stuart, he urged the discontinuance of quicklime in any future prison burial.

The findings at Newcastle, alongside those at Newgate in London and several other prisons that had been closed in the early 20th century, led to lasting changes in the method and rules surrounding burial within the prison walls. Amongst these provisions was the banning of quicklime, the provision of perforated holes in the ends of the coffin and the removal of clothing, 'except the shirt or similar garment'.

Neither Bell, Nor Candle: The Secret Reinterments

Following the completion of the exhumation and the investigative work, the bodies were ordered to be reburied at All Saints Cemetery, Jesmond, and great lengths were taken to avoid any public intervention or remembrance of the bodies. One Prison Commission report proposed that whilst a plan of the graves should be given to Newcastle Council, they should 'not' receive the 'Register of Graves which gives the name of prisoners and dates of executions.'

Reporting on the eventual reinterment, the *Aberdeen Press and Journal*, under the tongue in cheek headline, 'All Saints' Cemetery?' detailed the clandestine operation, 'In the darkness of the night and at an hour kept strictly secret the bodies of the murderers which lie in the precinct of Newcastle Gaol are to be taken up and reinterred in All Saints' Cemetery.' The bodies were reburied with 'neither bell, book nor candle…vouchsafed them, since no service will be held.' A final disgrace that reflected the history of punishment long after death.

Reporting on the reinterment, one newspaper quoted an unnamed prison official,

'It is strange, but in one custom we are more barbarous than our ancestors in bygone days. It is the toll of the Felon's Plot…Prison Officials who have assisted in the last act of a murder drama will agree that it is a mournful business.'

There was one final twist to the tale. In September 1928, *The Boston Guardian* carried the following story, 'Remains of a man who had been executed were found during excavation work for an automatic telephone exchange on the site of the old Newcastle Gaol.' This report tallies with one of the memories that was sent to the Newcastle Gaol Project team from a member of the public, Marie McNichol. Marie McNichol's grandfather John (Jack) Level was part of the demolition and excavation team working on the prison site. He was employed by Purdie, Lumsden & Co as a crane operator. Marie remembers that the building work was severely delayed when a body was uncovered 'wrapped in oilskins, like that of a sailor.' An investigation followed that delayed the excavation work considerably and on 27 August 1928 the *Yorkshire Post* reported that the body had remained unidentified but 'It is believed the remains are those of another executed man. The bones were reinterred at Jesmond on Saturday.'

All Saints Cemetery, Jesmond.

The exact location of the bodies in All Saints Cemetery is still a mystery and until 2022 there was no marker for the burials. As part of the project on the history of Newcastle Gaol that led to this book, a plaque was commissioned to memorialise the names of the executed men which was placed near the entrance of All Saints Cemetery, Jesmond. On the morning of 24 November, 2021, it was unveiled in the presence of distant relatives of the executed. Although remembered on the plaque, the bodies of Samuel Emery, Mark Sherwood, Patrick Forbes and William Row(e) remain unaccounted for.

Despite the scandal surrounding the evidence from the burials at Newcastle Gaol, the punishment of burial within the prison walls was still the subject of debate in the House of Commons as late as the 1960s. Reflecting on the punishment, the member of Parliament for Leeds West, Charles Pannel, wrote

'It is curious to discover that people thought that both private execution and private burial, and certainly the ignominy of burial such as this, would be a great deterrent. Nobody would take that view today. We would look upon the burying of a body in quicklime within the precincts of a prison wall rather as something completely ghoulish and out of keeping with our time.'

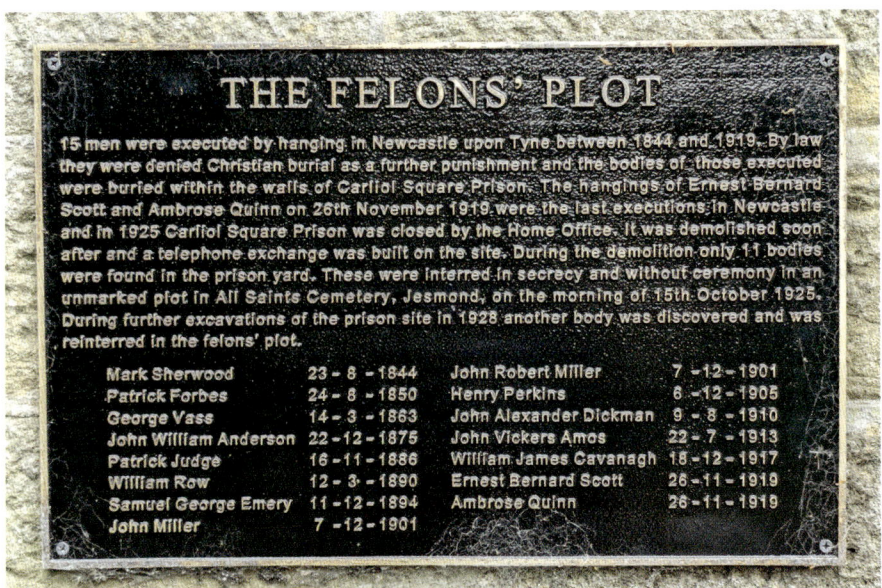

Plaque in All Saints Cemetery, Jesmond.

Conclusion

In many ways, the fate of the executed prisoners mirrored that of the prison that had once housed them. Despite its grand, imposing presence in the city for almost a century, it has left little or no trace and remains unmarked and, until recently, largely unknown to most residents. To find out why we now turn to its closure and the redevelopment of the area of East Pilgrim Street.

CHAPTER 8

'It is built as though it were meant to withstand a siege'

'We live in an age when such elaborate apparatus against violence and crime is not necessary'

DEMOLITION AND BEYOND

Reconstructing the Prison

As part of this book, the digital heritage company New Visions Heritage was commissioned to use Dobson's plans to digitally reconstruct the prison. Working on these plans was an opportunity to understand the prison layout and how it fitted within the town. With different types of plans surviving - from ink sketches to detailed architectural drafts - the challenge was to cross reference these for accuracy and likely development of the prison site. Some of the drawings included useful dimensions and details, while others were contradictory.

The patchy survival of plans of the site caused complications during the 3D reconstruction. With no site sections or elevations showing relationships between the different buildings, these had to be estimated using the slope of the existing hill at Carliol Square. New Visions Heritage used a photograph from the archives, probably taken in September 1925; this view, from the north west looking over the Prison, was crucial in enabling the buildings to be positioned at a correct relative height to each other. In the photo the steeple of St Cuthbert's church on Melbourne Street and a chimney of the electric supply station near Manors Station are clearly visible. These were invaluable as the relative location of these structures were key points to verifying the accuracy of the reconstruction.

There are a few other photographs available, including one looking down the street towards the gatehouse, and some images from a newspaper that show details of the later Prison, such as the exercise yard and area between the main building and the men's ward. These are unfortunately of low quality. They do, however, highlight a discrepancy between the drawings and the reality of the wall to the west of the men's ward as well as showing details such as the bricked-up top windows in the main building chapel, and the walkway between the men's ward and the chapel. Another discovery that digital visualisation methods brought to light was a moat-like lower-level area which was built to take account of the slope down towards Manors. The area at the back

New Visions Heritage's 3D reconstruction of the Prison.

of the prison hospital was of particular interest, as it suggested the location of the so-called 'execution shed.' Some plans showed this room to be an annex of the men's ward, built over the lower-level area that surrounds the building, which would have given a ready-made drop for executions. An old photograph of the hospital, along with the detailed design plans and elevations of the building, facilitated a detailed reconstruction of this area. This rendered view was of importance as it was in the basement of the hospital building that condemned prisoners would be kept awaiting the day of execution. It is only as a result of this digital reconstruction that we can now say that on their final day they would have had to walk up the stairs from the basement cells and out of the main hospital door, along the edge of the exercise yard and finally to the small room, or shed, attached to the southern end of the men's ward where the execution took place.

The Prison was in operation for less than a hundred years, however during this time it underwent a series of rebuilds and improvements, some of which were in response to changing practices in prison design and administration. Being able to compile the layout drawings into a chronological order offered insight into the phased development of the site. As discussed previously, the initial radial design for the Gaol envisaged six wings rather than the five that were built. In later years the eastern ward of cells was demolished allowing for the north most half of the men's ward to be built. This was later extended to the south, with the addition of new cells and a fabulous spiral staircase facing south, inviting light to flood into the central atrium space.

Another interesting detail that could not be picked up from photographs, but was hinted at in one of the earliest sketches of the Gaol, was the inclusion of the town's coat of arms above the main gate. Objects such as the coat of arms are particularly tricky and time consuming to model accurately. To create this part of the reconstruction we drew on other examples of the coat of arms and one in particular which survives on a street just off the Quayside, to create a model in 3D for the reconstruction.

Alongside the architectural drawings and photographs, the only other evidence we had to help with the reconstruction of the prison was a sketch made in 1826 and Dobson's painting. Both the painting and the sketch are illustrations of the view looking through the gate towards the Governor's house, but both include some degree of artistic licence with some details and proportions exaggerated for effect.

In creating the final visualisations revealed in this book, the artistic concept behind the interpretations was to keep them within a similar style, illustrative and evocative with lowish sun casting long shadows in the depths of the prison grounds, rather than present fully photorealistic interpretations. It was important for the final images to convey a feeling of the domineering and oppressive architecture, covered with soot, and weathering relevant to age and social context, therefore enhancing the mood of the illustrations and evoking the desired impression. The artistic decisions were taken to understand and appreciate the design, layout and relationship of the buildings in addition to the dramatic changes that occurred to the Prison during its near 100 year lifetime.

Conclusion

In September 1925 a local newspaper reported that a group of 'keen faced business men' were taking stock of Newcastle Prison, trying to estimate the cost of removing this 'gloomy pile'.

'The men who designed and built the gaol must have been people of great thoroughness. It is built as though it were meant to withstand a siege, and in the strength and grimness of its aspect it cannot have failed to exercise an awe-inspiring effect upon successive generations. We live in an age when such elaborate apparatus against violence and crime is not necessary. The gaol had become an anachronism in the midst of a well-behaved and peaceable city… and so its career has been terminated'.

The same month, a public auction was held in the exercise yard and over 800 lots were sold, including the semi-circular chapel, two organs, and a Roman Catholic altar. Newspapers reported that 'women visitors' bought up domestic and kitchen articles while others purchased spoons 'once used for the "forcible-feeding" of obstreperous prisoners'. This was an ignominious end for a building once heralded as more of a 'palace' than a prison.

One of the main problems with the Prison from its inception was the relentless rate of urban development around it. At 1.8 acres [7284 square metres], the prison site was smaller than a football pitch and, in the midst of the busy pubs and tenements surrounding Carliol Square, was Erick Street, Newcastle's red-light district. Meanwhile, from as early as the 1830s, the district of Manors was earmarked as a potential railway hub. In 1836 the builder and planner Richard Grainger proposed a railway line from North Shields to Newcastle that would run alongside the prison, rather than arriving into the centre of town via Quayside or Pilgrim Street. In the 1840s John Dobson designed some of the local railway infrastructure and his Manors Station building was just over 164 feet [50 metres] south east of the prison walls.

Alongside the noise of passenger trains and passing freight, the prisoners were disturbed by the 'pandemonium' of the Carliol Fair every year. They would have also heard children playing in the yard of the Dobson-designed Jubilee School a mere 26 feet [8 metres] from the walls. By the mid 1920s, city authorities were planning new north/south thoroughfares. With a new road planned to connect City Road and Barras Bridge, the Prison stood out in a district busy with manufacturing and transport infrastructure.

The closure of the Prison in 1925 coincided with regeneration of the district east of Pilgrim Street. Despite spending enormous sums of money on the Prison since 1822, the Council decided to purchase the site from the Home Office and, although other projects were mooted, a building named Telephone House was built on the site to house a telephone exchange. Around the same time Carliol House opened on the corner of Pilgrim Street and Market Street. This Art Deco-inspired structure was purpose-built to house the North Eastern Electricity Supply Company. A few years later the new Central Police and Fire Station opened opposite Carliol House. In a striking sign of the old making way for the new, stones taken from the walls of the demolished prison ended up supporting the foundations of the Tyne Bridge, which was opened in 1928.

Despite the building boom of the 1920s, the East Pilgrim Street district became dominated by swathes of road construction associated with the Swan House roundabout and Central Motorway, in the 1960s and 70s. In this brutalist vision of motorways, car parks, and walkways in the sky, older buildings like the Holy Jesus Hospital and All Saints Church were hidden by car traffic, making centuries of foot traffic from Pilgrim Street to Quayside a distant memory. While Telephone House still stands, Carliol House was mostly demolished in 2023 to make way for a new headquarters for His Majesty's Revenue and Customs (HMRC). The Central Police and Fire Station, disused since 2014, was converted into a luxury hotel in 2025. It is clear that this district of Newcastle is undergoing a transformation which resembles that of the 1920s in scale and impact.

Since the construction of Telephone House, the occupants of the building in Carliol Square have been many and varied. The building served as Newcastle's telephone exchange for several decades before other tenants moved in, including a coffee shop, dance studios, tattoo parlour, and World Headquarters nightclub. In a curious historical twist, one of the main tenants in Telephone House today is 'ReCoCo' (Recovery College Collective), a charity which hosts activities, training, engagement, and support for people encountering difficulties related to mental health, addiction, poverty, disability, and complex family situations. In stark contrast to Newcastle Prison, which held tens of thousands of prisoners with scant regard for their wellbeing, ReCoCo provides an alternative model of care that is focused on supporting people perceived to be on the margins of society. The staff are keenly aware of the space they inhabit, and of the histories of crime and punishment that resonate around them like a faintly audible hum. Aerial views of Carliol Square indicate that the footprint of the prison neatly matches the size and scale of Telephone House. This is a reminder that the ghosts of Newcastle Prison still haunt passers-by at the centenary of its closure.

These new digital reconstructions enhance our knowledge of the Prison, alongside the few surviving original photographs.

One of the few known photographs showing the Prison.

A modern photograph from a drone, showing the prison site.

Glossary

Assizes The Assizes were court sessions held in England and Wales to administer justice in serious criminal and civil cases. They were presided over by travelling judges who visited counties on a circuit, typically twice a year. These courts were the most senior level of local justice. The Assizes system lasted until 1972, when it was replaced by the Crown Court under the Courts Act 1971, centralising criminal justice.

Borstal The Borstal system was established under the Prevention of Crime Act 1908. Borstals aimed to rehabilitate young offenders aged 16-21 rather than punish, focusing on education, discipline, and vocational training. Borstals were seen as an alternative to traditional prisons, which were deemed unsuitable for young offenders.

Cheveux de frise A set of revolving spikes on the prison wall consisting of a row of closely spaced vertical iron or steel spikes or bars designed to deter or impede anyone trying to breach the wall.

Common Prostitute A 'common prostitute' was legally defined as a woman who habitually engaged in prostitution, leading her to be treated as a social and moral deviant. Such women were frequently subject to punitive measures, including imprisonment, to control what was considered public vice.

Death Recorded 'Death recorded' was a legal term used when a judge recorded a death sentence as required by law, but with the intention to pardon or commute the sentence.

House of Correction A House of Correction was a type of penal institution used from the 16th to the 19th centuries. Designed to punish and reform minor offenders, particularly those convicted of vagrancy, petty crimes, or moral offences, these facilities aimed to instill discipline and work ethic. Unlike prisons for more serious crimes, Houses of Correction were focused on rehabilitation through work and punishment. They evolved into larger prison systems, and their role diminished with the rise of more formal incarceration practices.

Hopping A hopping was a general name for a fair. It is thought that the name derived from the dancing that took place.

John Howard (1726–90) was an English prison reformer known for his contributions to improving the conditions of prisons in the 18th century. Horrified by squalid and inhumane conditions he dedicated his life to advocating for better sanitation, nutrition, and treatment of prisoners. The State of the Prisons in England and Wales (1777) set out his findings from inspections across Europe and called for reforms, influencing policies on prison management.

Keelmen The Keelmen of Tyne and Wear were so called because they operated keels—large, shallow-draft boats used to transport coal from the riverbanks to collier ships. Due to the shallow waters of the River Tyne, larger vessels were unable to navigate upstream to collect coal directly from the riverside. This necessity led to the use of keels to ferry coal to waiting ships. In 1699 the Keelmen decided to raise funds to build a hospital for sick and retired keelmen and their families. It was opened in 1701 and still stands to this day.

Larceny Larceny was the theft of personal property, with penalties varying by value of the property stolen. Simple larceny could lead to imprisonment or transportation, while grand larceny might result in life imprisonment or capital punishment. Larceny laws were strict, reflecting society's deep concern over property rights.

Life preserver A thick cane, about a foot long, with a ball of lead attached to one end by catgut netting and fastened to the wrist by a leather strap at the other.

Mug Shot In the nineteenth century, a 'mug shot' was known as a 'police photograph' or 'criminal likeness'. The images were used for identifying arrested or suspected individuals. The practice of taking photographs started in the mid-to-late 1800s as part of criminal identification systems.

Murder Act 1751 The Murder Act 1751 was brought about owing, in part, to a perceived mid-century crime wave in London. The Act stated that 'for better preventing the horrid crime of murder… some further terror and peculiar mark of infamy be added to the punishment.'

Panopticon A panopticon prison is designed with a central watchtower surrounded by cells, allowing guards to observe inmates without them knowing if they are being watched, thus fostering a sense of constant surveillance. This architectural design, conceived by Jeremy Bentham, aimed to induce self-discipline among prisoners due to the psychological effect of potential observation.

Phrenology Phrenology emerged in the eighteenth century and was an 'analytical science' that linked the shape of the human skull with certain mental faculties. Originally devised by Viennese physician Franz Joseph Gall (1758-1828), it became a hugely 'popular science' in the eighteenth and nineteenth centuries. The leading Scottish phrenologist, George Combe, gave sell out talks at Newcastle's Literary and Philosophical Society and visited the gaol.

Pinioning Pinioning was undertaken by the executioner. The convicts' hands and later, ankles, were strapped or tied with rope. This was to prevent prisoners moving on the gallows platform or struggling, which could lead to a botched hanging. This procedure often took place in a separate room of the prison to the execution chamber.

Silent System The Silent System was a penal policy designed to isolate prisoners and enforce silence for reflection and reform. Inmates were prohibited from speaking to one another, and their daily routines were strictly regulated. They were confined to individual cells, where they spent the majority of their time in solitude. The system proved controversial, as prolonged isolation often led to mental health breakdown.

Solitary System The Solitary System was a method of prison management that focused on isolating prisoners in individual cells for the majority of their sentence. Unlike the Silent System, which still allowed some interaction, the Solitary System aimed to provide complete solitude, with prisoners having little to no contact with others. The goal was to encourage reflection, remorse, and self-discipline, believing that isolation would lead to reform.

Ticket of leave man An individual who had been granted a conditional release from prison before completing their full sentence. The conditions attached to the ticket typically included requirements for good behaviour, regular reporting to authorities, and restrictions on movement. This allowed for a gradual reintegration of convicts into society.

Transportation Transportation, historically, refers to a punishment where convicted criminals were sent to America or Australia to serve their sentence, often for offences where the death sentence was considered too severe. The felons were sentenced to either a term of years or life, after which they could return home at their own expense or remain in the colony as free individuals.

Treadwheel A treadwheel, or treadmill, was a rotating wheel which was powered by prisoners climbing steps on the wheel. This was pointless hard labour and exhausting exercise aligned with the theory of atonement through work.

Turning Queens / King's Evidence A legal term that refers to a situation where an individual, often a co-defendant or accomplice, decides to testify against their fellow criminals.

Suggestions for Further Reading

Allan Brodie, Jane Croom and James O Davies. *English Prisons: An Architectural History* (Swindon: English Heritage, 2002).

Rosalind Crone. *Guide to the Criminal Prisons of Nineteenth-Century England* (London: London Publishing Partnership, 2018).

John J Eddlestone. *Murderous Tyneside: The Executed of the Twentieth Century* (Derby: Breedon, 1997).

Michelle Higgs. *Prison Life in Victorian England* (Stroud: Tempus, 2007).

Patrick Low, Helen Rutherford and Clare Sandford-Couch eds. *Execution in Nineteenth-Century Britain: From Public Spectacle to Hidden Ritual* (London: Routledge, 2020).

Shane McCorristine. *William Corder and the Red Barn Murder: Journeys of the Criminal Body* (Basingstoke: Palgrave, 2014).

Gwenda Morgan and Peter Rushton. *Rogues, Thieves and the Rule of Law: The Problem of Law Enforcement in North-East England, 1718-1800* (London: UCL Press, 1998).

Norval Morris and David J Rothman. *The Oxford History of the Prison: The Practice of Punishment in Western Society* (New York and Oxford: Oxford University Press, 1995).

Philip Priestley. *Victorian Prison Lives: English Prison Biography, 1830-1914* (London: Pimlico, 1999).

Barry Redfern. *The Gallows Tree: Crime and Punishment in Eighteenth-Century Northumberland and Berwick-upon-Tweed* (Newcastle: Tyne Bridge Publishing, 2013).

Barry Redfern. *Victorian Villains: Prisoners from Newcastle Gaol, 1871-1873* (Newcastle: Tyne Bridge Publishing, 2006).

Neil R Story. *Prisons and Prisoners in Victorian Britain* (Stroud: The History Press, 2010).

David Wilson. *Pain and Retribution: A Short History of British Prisons, 1066 to the Present* (London: Reaktion Books, 2014).

Appendix

Executions of inmates of Newcastle Prison

NAME	DATE OF EXECUTION	CRIME	LOCATION
Jane Jamieson	7 March, 1829	Murder	Town Moor
Mark Sherwood	23 August, 1844	Murder	Town Moor
Patrick Forbes	24 August, 1850	Murder	Newcastle Gaol
George Vass	14 March, 1863	Murder	Newcastle Gaol
John William Anderson	22 December, 1875	Murder	Newcastle Gaol
Patrick Judge	16 November, 1886	Murder	HMP Newcastle
William Row(e)	12 March, 1890	Murder	HMP Newcastle
Samuel George Emery	11 December, 1894	Murder	HMP Newcastle
John Miller	7 December, 1901	Murder	HMP Newcastle
John Robert Miller	7 December, 1901	Murder	HMP Newcastle
Henry Perkins	6 December, 1905	Murder	HMP Newcastle
John Alexander Dickman	9 August, 1910	Murder	HMP Newcastle
John Vickers Amos	22 July, 1913	Murder	HMP Newcastle
William James Cavanagh	18 December, 1917	Murder	HMP Newcastle
Ernest Bernard Scott	26 November, 1919	Murder	HMP Newcastle
Ambrose Quinn	26 November, 1919	Murder	HMP Newcastle

Governors of Newcastle Gaol

James Sopwith 1828 - 29
Gilbert Grey 1830 - 36
Samuel Thompson 1836 - 60
Thomas Robins 1860 - 80
William Wookey 1881 - 94
Roderick Dhu Glenlyon Hamilton Burgoyne 1894 - 99
James Osmond Nelson 1899 - 1900
William Makepeace Thackeray Synge c.1900
Harry Bartle 1901 - 10
Henry John Heller 1910 - 15
Frank Walter Gibson 1916 - 18
John Hallesey (Acting Governor) 1919 - 20
Frank Thomas Reynolds 1921 - 23
Herbert Pickering 1923 - 24
Edward Gerald French 1924 - 25

Illustration Credits

CHAPTER 1: INTRODUCTION

CHAPTER HEADER PAGE: GATEWAY OF THE GAOL, John Dobson (c.1828), Tyne & Wear Archives, NEM

MUGSHOT OF JOHN ROMAN (c.1873). Tyne & Wear Archives, NEM
MUGSHOT OF ROSANNA WATSON (c.1873), Tyne & Wear Archives, NEM
MUGSHOT OF PATRICK O'NEILL (c.1873). Tyne & Wear Archives, NEM
EXECUTION OF ALLEGED WITCHES IN NEWCASTLE, 1650, Wikimedia Commons
'VIEW FROM THE NORTH OF THE GATE OF THAT TOWN CALLED NEWGATE' (1781), Newcastle Libraries
GRAND PLAN FOR A DESIGN FOR A COUNTY PRISON. Thomas Sopwith, *A Treatise on Isometrical Drawing*, 2nd ed., (1838)
DETAIL OF CARLIOL CROFT, from Charles Hutton, *A Plan of Newcastle upon Tyne and Gateshead* (1770). Newcastle University Library, Special Collections
PLAN OF THE NEW PRISONS IN NEWCASTLE (c.1828), Tyne & Wear Archives, NEM
GATEWAY OF THE GAOL, John Dobson (c.1828), Tyne & Wear Archives, NEM
NORTH WEST VIEW OF GAOL IN 1828, New Visions Heritage
FOUNDATION PLAQUE (1823), Tyne & Wear Archives, NEM
BLOCK PLAN, 1860s, New Visions Heritage
INTERNAL SPIRAL STAIRCASE, 1860s, New Visions Heritage
BIRDS-EYE VIEW OF GAOL, 1860s, INSIDE THE PRISON - Visualisation and photograph from 1925, New Visions Heritage/Newcastle City Library
EXERCISE YARD Newcastle City Library

POP-OUT NEWGATE STREET PETITION (c.1827), National Library of Scotland
POP-OUT SANDGATE IN 1856 c.1898, Newcastle City Library

CHAPTER 2: LIFE INSIDE NEWCASTLE GAOL

CHAPTER HEADER PAGE: LINE DRAWING OF THE GAOL ENTRANCE: Richardson's *Descriptive Companion thro' Newcastle Upon Tyne and its Vicinity* (1838)

POSTCARD OF THE TOWN FROM THE AIR The Aircraft Manufacturing Company Limited (nd)
CHAPEL AT LINCOLN CASTLE Postcard (nd)
CHAPEL AT PENTONVILLE Henry Mayhew and John Binny, *The Criminal Prisons of London and Scenes from Prison Life* (1862)
OAKUM ROOM, COLDBATH FIELDS Henry Mayhew and John Binny, *The*

Criminal Prisons of London and Scenes from Prison Life (1862)
WHIPPING POST IN WANDSWORTH Henry Mayhew and John Binny, *The Criminal Prisons of London and Scenes from Prison Life* (1862)
VIEW OF THE PRISON Newcastle City Libraries
BOYS EXERCISING TOTHILL FIELDS Henry Mayhew and John Binny, *The Criminal Prisons of London and Scenes from Prison Life* (1862)
DEBTORS CELL, G.B. Richardson Newcastle City Library
COUNTESS OF DERWENTWATER, *The Monthly Chronicle of Law and Legend* (1888)

POP OUT THE NEWCASTLE CORONER *The Blue Book* (1925), Newcastle City Libraries

CHAPTER 3 GAOL STAFF

CHAPTER HEADER PAGE: DETAIL FROM NEWCASTLE PRISON OFFICIALS', *Illustrated Chronicle* (31 March 1925)

'NEWCASTLE PRISON OFFICIALS', *Illustrated Chronicle* (31 March 1925)
PLAN OF GAOL HIGHLIGHTING GOVERNOR'S ACCOMMODATION
PLAN OF GAOL HIGHLIGHTING CHAPEL LOCATION
DUTIES OF THE KEEPERS & MATRONS, EXTRACT FROM ADDITIONAL RULES FOR THE GAOL AND HOUSE OF CORRECTION 1830 - Author photograph - Tyne & Wear Archives, NEM
PLAN OF GAOL HIGHLIGHTING MATRON'S ACCOMMODATION
CHIEF WARDER AT THE PENTONVILLE PRISON AND PRINCIPAL MATRON AT THE FEMALE CONVICT PRISON, BRIXTON, Henry Mayhew and John Binny, *The Criminal Prisons of London and Scenes from Prison Life* (1862))
ASSISTANT TURNKEY & SALARY - Newcastle Gaol Records (1837) - Author photograph - Tyne & Wear Archives, NEM

POP OUT 'CAP OF MAINTENANCE' - Author photograph - reproduced with kind permission of the Mayor's Office. Newcastle City Council
POP OUT GOVERNOR MAJOR JAMES OSMOND NELSON - *Alderley & Wilmslow Advertiser* (1912), British Newspaper Archive
POP OUT THE REV WILLIAM FAITHFULL LUMLEY - British Newspaper Archive
POP OUT 4 – 5 RAVENSWORTH TERRACE, NEWCASTLE – Flickr

CHAPTER 4: THE WOMEN'S GAOL

CHAPTER HEADER PAGE: PHOTO OF MARY ERSKINE CHRISTIE Tyne & Wear Archives, NEM

PLAN OF THE GAOL – HIGHLIGHTING THE WOMEN'S WING
FEMALE CONVICTS AND THEIR CHILDREN IN CONVICT PRISON EXERCISE YARD Henry Mayhew and John Binny, *The Criminal Prisons of*

London and Scenes from Prison Life (1862)
THE FEMALE FACTORY FROM PROCTOR'S QUARRY, DETAIL SHOWING THE CASCADES FEMALE FACTORY IN HOBART, VAN DIEMAN'S LAND (1844) John Skinner Prout (1805-1876) – Wikimedia, Public Domain
TYPICAL SINGLE CELL IN A VICTORIAN-ERA GAOL, PORT ARTHUR PENAL SETTLEMENT, TASMANIA Author photograph
FEMALE CONVICTS ON LAUNDRY DUTY Henry Mayhew and John Binny, *The Criminal Prisons of London and Scenes from Prison Life* (1862)
NEWCASTLE GENERAL POST OFFICE ON ST NICHOLAS' STREET, NEWCASTLE Author photograph
SCOLDS' BRIDLE Author photograph, Newcastle Keep

POP OUT IMAGE OF THE WOMEN'S WING, New Visions Heritage
POP OUT IMAGE OF YOUNG OFFENDER Tyne & Wear Archives, NEM
POP OUT CONSTANCE LYTTON Creative Commons CC0 1.0

CHAPTER 5: ESCAPES

CHAPTER HEADER PAGE: JACK SHEPPARD HELPING AN ACCOMPLICE ESCAPE USING KNOTTED SHEETS - CHEVEUX DE FRISE IN FOREGROUND London Museum

PRISONER IN SCOTCH BONNET CAP Henry Mayhew, *The Criminal Prisons of London and Scenes from Prison Life* (1862)
IMAGE OF PRISON Newcastle Libraries
JACK SHEPPARD HELPING AN ACCOMPLICE ESCAPE USING KNOTTED SHEETS - CHEVEUX DE FRISE IN FOREGROUND London Museum
THE WARRIOR PRISON HULK Henry Mayhew, *The Criminal Prisons of London and Scenes from Prison Life* (1862)
JOHANN JURGEN KUHR British Newspaper Archive

POP OUT ETCHING OF CHIEF CONSTABLE ELLIOT from the *Monthly Chronicle of North-Country Lore and Legend* (1891)
POP OUT JACK SHEPPARD engraving by George White based on a painting by James Thornhill (1728)

CHAPTER 6: EXECUTIONS

DICKMAN TRIAL *Illustrated Police News* (16 July 1910)
JANE JAMIESON AT HER TRIAL Newcastle University Special Collections
KEELMEN'S HOSPITAL c.1800, Newcastle Libraries
THE OLD FISH MARKET, SANDHILL, NEWCASTLE UPON TYNE, c.1826-1830 HENRY PERLEE PARKER (1795–1873) North East Museums (Laing)
ARMSTRONG'S 1769 MAP SHOWING GALLOWS Creative Commons

SANDGATE PANT, 1890, Newcastle Libraries
TOWN MOOR RACECOURSE MAP & GRANDSTAND *Oliver's Map of Newcastle* 1930 Newcastle Libraries
GEORGE VASS IN HIS CELL 1863 Newcastle University Special Collections
ERNEST BERNARD SCOTT IN THE CHARGE OF DETECTIVE ANDREWS & AMBROSE QUINN, *Illustrated Chronicle* (12 August 1919)
MURDER OF A NORTHUMBERLAND MINER *The Illustrated Police News* (August 1919)
HANGMAN JAMES BERRY Author's collection
JOHN MILLERS AND JOHN ROBERT MILLER IN COURT
'THE ACCUSED A SKETCH IN COURT', *Newcastle Evening Chronicle* (15 Nov 1901)

POP OUT RICHARD LOWRY *Newcastle Chronicle* (2 Nov 1899)
POP OUT ALEXANDER INGRAM - *Illustratred Police News* (28 Oct 1911)
POP OUT JOHN ALEXANDER DICKMAN'S PIGEON *Illustrated Police News* (16 July 1910)

CHAPTER 7: BURIAL & POST-MORTEM PUNISHMENT

CHAPTER HEADER PAGE: GALLOWS DRAWING SKIN PORTION FROM 'AN ACCOUNT OF THE EXECUTION OF CHARLES SMITH 1817', Newcastle Libraries

ST ANDREW'S CHURCH Newcastle Libraries
EXECUTION CERTIFICATE PATRICK JUDGE 1886 Author's collection
BARBER SURGEONS, CERTIFICATE. Newcastle University Special Collections
CHARLES SMITH 'SKIN BOOK' *An Account of the Execution of Charles Smith 1817* Newcastle Libraries
DISSECTION LECTURES ADVERT FOR JANE JAMIESON ANATOMICAL DEMONSTRATIONS ADVERT, (7 March 1829), Newcastle University Special Collections
BALLAST HILLS BODY SNATCHING BROADSIDE Tyne & Wear Archives, NEM
INSPECTOR VIEWING DESCERATED STONE WITH INITIALS NEWCASTLE PRISON, *North Daily Mail, Newcastle Chronicle* (3 Sept 1925)
ALL SAINT'S CEMETERY, JESMOND Newcastle Libraries
FELONS' PLOT PLAQUE, ALL SAINT'S CEMETERY, JESMOND Author photograph

POP OUT MURDER ACT 1751 WILLIAM HOGARTH, THE REWARD OF CRUELTY (PLATE IV FROM 'THE FOUR STAGES OF CRUELTY', 1751). Creative Commons
POP OUT JOHN FIFE – Author's collection
POP OUT BURKE AND HARE c1850, Wikimedia
POP OUT SOPHIA QUIN/ROSANNA ROX OLD HOUSES AT THE HEAD OF THE SIDE, 1874, Newcastle Libraries
POP OUT BUCKET LEG Heather Bigg, *Artificial Limbs: And the*

Amputations which Afford the most Appropriate Stumps in Civil and Military Surgery, (1885)

CHAPTER 8: DEMOLITION AND BEYOND

IMAGE OF THE PRISON New Visions Heritage
IMAGE OF THE PRISON New Visions Heritage
MODERN IMAGE OF PRISON SITE Hellow.co